A PURPOSEFUL LIFE

www.penguin.co.uk

A PURPOSEFUL LIFE

What I've learned about breaking barriers
and inspiring change

DAWN BUTLER

torva

TRANSWORLD PUBLISHERS
Penguin Random House, One Embassy Gardens,
8 Viaduct Gardens, London sw11 7bw
www.penguin.co.uk

Transworld is part of the Penguin Random House group of companies
whose addresses can be found at global.penguinrandomhouse.com

Penguin
Random House
UK

First published in Great Britain in 2023 by Torva
an imprint of Transworld Publishers

A CIP catalogue record for this book
is available from the British Library.

ISBN 9781911709329

Typeset in 14/17pt Granjon LT Std by Jouve (UK), Milton Keynes
Printed and bound in Great Britain by Clays Ltd, Elcograf S.p.A.

The authorized representative in the EEA is Penguin Random House Ireland,
Morrison Chambers, 32 Nassau Street, Dublin D02 YH68.

Penguin Random House is committed to a sustainable
future for our business, our readers and our planet. This book is made
from Forest Stewardship Council® certified paper.

CONTENTS

FOREWORD

Hey, Dad, guess what? Your little girl did it! I'm now an author.

I can almost see you looking down, a smile on your face, thinking, 'Of course you are!'

You always believed in me. You were my loudest cheerleader, even when I didn't quite understand why I needed one.

I miss you more than words could ever express, but this book has allowed me to journey back through countless stories, and as an adult I finally comprehend why you did the things you did. Well, most of them.

I'll never forget the day I found myself in tears because someone had accused me of lying. You, with your Jamaican accent, told me, 'Stop cry and fix up yuhself, dem is di one who should be crying.'

You and Mum laid a solid foundation, creating a world where, even if I faltered, there was always a soft, warm safety net to catch me. As a result, there's nothing I believe I cannot do. When others call me strong, I proudly say that my resilience is not just strength, it's survival. I inherited this from my parents. There is so much that I now embrace, which has enabled me to be fearless as a disruptor.

We are all looking after Mum – losing someone after over fifty years together isn't easy and she is often very tearful. She misses you dearly.

They say a daughter's first love is her father, and I never fully understood the depth of that truth until the day I could no longer cuddle up to you and hear your voice.

Thank you, Dad. I miss you.

INTRODUCTION

Apparently I'm responsible for one of the most powerful political moments of 2021, which led to the downfall of Prime Minister Boris Johnson. It all started when I called him a liar in Parliament – that word, 'liar', is an important, loaded word for me, and I don't use it lightly. It goes against everything I stand for to watch someone lie again and again, especially when I know the truth. At the time, I was dismissed from the Commons and criticized for using 'unparliamentary language'. But a later privileges committee report found that Boris *did* deliberately mislead Parliament. If he hadn't resigned as an MP a few days earlier, it would have been the first time a former prime minister was thrown out of Parliament for lying. The very fabric of our society is being undermined by lies and fake news and I want to do my part in making it better. The stories in this book will explain why it's so important to me that we create a better world, with strong and connected communities.

A Purposeful Life takes you through stories of my own experiences from when I was eight years old, and going through the British school system, to my years as a computer programmer, my encounters with the police, my early days as a Labour MP for Brent South, one of only two Black female MPs in Parliament, and finally to my life-changing experience of breast cancer. Admittedly, the journey won't be easy or even comfortable, but I hope it inspires you to disrupt some aspect of your life or even your belief system. From one tale to another, I take a deep dive into the necessity of service and community, and understanding intersectionality, challenging our biases, and learning how to speak up and step into our power to bring on real and long-lasting change. There will be laughter (don't worry), and hope – maybe even some tears.

I hope that when you pick up this book you are ready to lean into your purpose. It will be unique to you. It could be anything from wanting to be the best parent and advocate for your child to becoming a better police officer, who no longer wants to keep quiet, a better doctor, who chooses to treat all their patients with care and respect, or even a better MP, who feels they could afford to speak a little louder. Maybe you want to be a better ally, a better neighbour or a better friend. Whatever it is, may this book inspire you to take on, in your own small way, one of many battles I present to you. There is a lot still to be done in these uncertain times but, most importantly, I can't do it all on my own, no matter how hard I try!

This book is about working to dismantle the many

archaic systems that we come up against throughout our lives, from schooling to government to health, that work only to serve the few, not the many. If these systems aren't willing to change, we must play a role in forcing that change. How can we create new, updated systems that consider the wealth of diversity that exists not just in London but the world? We need a revolution, a structural rewriting in which we reduce inequality and centre justice and fairness. When I was younger, my parents taught me to be resilient and my brothers gave me tools to be resistant. Now it's time to complete the power of three. It is time for a revolution.

We all need hope in our lives, and the acronym I like to use for that word is: Help Other People Exceed. One of the best ways to do this is to welcome those things that we fear or find challenging so that we can gain a new set of skills or enhance our abilities. No one is beyond learning and growing – in fact, it's integral to achieving our potential and becoming more accepting and compassionate human beings. I have deliberately designed this book with wide margins, and there is room at the back so that you can make notes – for you, not for me, although as you will gather, I have a growth mindset so quite like feedback! As you read, you may be reminded of a situation you have experienced, or learn a new way of dealing with conflict or criticism. I would love you to discuss and debate parts of the book with me. It has been a labour of love, written at a time when I was recovering from cancer. It has helped me, and I hope it will help you too.

I

COCKROACHES DON'T FLY

THE FIRST TIME I WAS EVER called a liar I was eight. It's one of the most prominent memories I have as a Black schoolkid growing up in Leytonstone, East London in the seventies, an area of wide-boys and skinheads, Africans and Caribbeans. The school holidays were over, and I had come back from a trip to Jamaica to see extended family. Mum and Dad would have worked hard to save up for it, and they took me with them as I was too young to be left behind with my brothers and sister. I was keen to share with the class something scary but maybe even exciting that I had seen while I was away. Teachers used to ask what we had done during the school holidays, so when my turn came, I stood in front of the room and said, 'Miss, I went to Jamaica, and I saw a cockroach that flew!'

'Cockroaches don't fly,' she said emphatically.

'Yeah, yeah, but I saw it. I saw it fly across the room!'

But my teacher, impatient, insisted I was lying. I stood there, frozen to the spot, trying to work out what was happening. Where was the excitement? What about the questions? I recalled the outdoor toilets, the floor shifting beneath me, the torch I was told to bring along, and the cockroaches crawling everywhere. When one of them flew towards me, I was petrified and ran, forgetting to go to the loo. Instead I went back to my room where I stayed awake for a very long time. After that I never went to the loo alone for the entire trip.

I shared the story because the memory of how I felt was one of the main things I remembered from my holiday. I could have told the story of how I made friends with a goat and talked to it every day to amuse myself. One day, rather than rushing out to greet my friendly goat, I was told to wait inside. But I was a stubborn little thing and decided to look at what was happening. To my horror, they killed the goat, my friend, and cooked it for dinner. I swore then that I would never eat curried goat, and to this day, I never have. Or I could have told the story of how I ate so many mangoes that I had to be rushed to the hospital because of the amount of sugar in my blood. But I chose to share the cockroach story because it was out of the ordinary. I thought the class would want to know more, but my teacher's reaction confused me. From her point of view, there was nothing more to be said on the subject: that was the end of it. She had never experienced it, therefore I must have been making it up. I could feel the whole class looking at me, probably laughing, because the teacher had told them I was lying. The tears started to build.

'Sit down,' she said, 'or stand outside the door.' This was the punishment for naughty kids. Often the head teacher would patrol the corridors and send any children waiting there to her office. I opted to go outside, but I still couldn't work out how to express myself to this adult or convince her of the truth. At the time, I wished I had known not to let anyone, even an adult, shift me from my own knowledge.

These days, children are taught to use words to defend themselves and to protect their boundaries, to try to speak out on discrimination or abuse – those tools weren't given to me back then. Instead my parents had taught me to find the safest and closest person to me when I needed help. So, instead of waiting for the head, I ran out of school and into the playground in search of my dad, the one person who could defend me when I couldn't defend myself. I climbed the playground fence and lowered myself on to Mrs Mavis's wall – she used to shout at me from the window, 'Get off my wall!' We laugh about this now. I ran across the road to my house, and sat on the front doorstep where my dad found me in tears. He was shocked to see me there as he had only just dropped me at school. I never learned what he said to my teacher that day, but she never called me a liar again.

*

I can recall a time during my career as an MP when a journalist asked me what it felt like to grow up poor. It took me aback because I didn't recognize that description of me and my family. The road my family lived on was a mix of mostly white and South Asian working-class families, with a handful of Black ones, the Butlers having been the first Black family to move into the area. It was a friendly road, and when I speak to the people I used to play with on our street we all reflect on how we thought everyone's street was like ours. Writing this book inspired me to contact the kids I used to play with, and we had a reunion. Richard, Jason, Edwin, Sean, Irma and I stopped outside Jennifer's old house and sang her happy birthday because she was unable to join us. This is a connection money can't buy.

It was clear that that journalist had misconceptions of the working class and maybe even of Blackness – there was obviously a preconceived narrative attached to the facts of my upbringing. We always had something to eat – we were never hungry – and we always had clothes on our backs. They weren't the most fashionable outfits, or the latest trends, but I never considered us to be poor. If anything, I considered us proud, and so were a lot of the working-class families I grew up with. Many were probably on lower incomes, but they were used to making a little stretch a long way. In today's climate, I think we should give more credit and respect to the working class of our country.

My dad, Milo, moved to London from Jamaica in the late 1950s, renting a room before relocating to what became our family home in Leytonstone. Arriving in London, he wondered why there were so many factories side by side on the road, not realizing they were houses with chimneys. For my dad – as it was for so many from the Caribbean – England was the motherland, paved with gold and all that. My parents came to London, invited by the British government, to help rebuild the country. Jamaica became independent in 1962, but as far as they were concerned England was home. Queen Elizabeth II was their head of state, so they never learned the Jamaican national anthem. When I was learning more about my parents' country of birth, I asked my dad to sing the national anthem with me. He sang, 'God save our gracious Queen . . .' and I sang, 'Eternal Father bless our land, guard us with thy mighty hand.' We cracked up, laughing, but it was a serious indication of how Britain was home to him.

My dad worked at the Matchbox toy car factory, then for the railways, and eventually, through a payment agreement that lasted years, bought the bakery he was working at (which he later named Butlers Bakery), although he never made any money from it. Dad was a jack-of-all-trades: cutting hair, baking bread, and playing in a band called Balance Power where he was the lead singer. He could also play drums, bass and keyboard. He performed gigs with his band all over the country but made sure to be home in the evenings to spend time with the family. In his spare time, he taught me how to play bass guitar in the cellar of our house, where he put egg boxes on the walls to soundproof his 'studio'. He used to sit me down and take me through the lyrics of a song, teaching me the importance of the words and the lessons to be found in them. My lifelong passion for justice, fairness and a peaceful co-existence between people and communities comes in the main from my dad, probably best exemplified through one of the band's album covers: a Black fist and a white fist balancing on scales.

The cellar was an important staple in my life. We had amazing parties down there, but it also held a massive secret. When my dad's friend divorced his wife and was homeless, my mum wouldn't allow my dad to put him up. So, when my mum went to bed, my dad would sneak him in to sleep, and when she left the house, my dad would let him have a shower. My brothers and I thought this was the funniest thing ever, and we kept that secret for months.

Dad was equal parts sarcastic, funny and tough. A parent once came to our house to complain about one of my older brothers, who had teased his son about his hair and said it needed combing. My dad stood at the door, listened for a while, looked at the boy's father, looked at the son, then asked him to wait. He went inside, got a comb, and handed it to him. My brother and I were at the top of the stairs, howling. That's not to say my brother didn't get into trouble, he did, but my dad still managed to make a joke of it.

On the flip side, my mum, Ambro, was the disciplinarian (even though she will absolutely deny it now). She came to join my dad in London after he'd saved enough to send for her. Mum juggled long hours as an auxiliary nurse while keeping house and making sure we were home on time from school. If we were ever late, she heard about it through the grapevine of our local community – there were no mobile phones yet. Our community was powerful and never skipped a beat, and many times I failed to get away with disobedience. For example, at school, we had a strict dress code, but on one occasion I thought I was clever enough to rebel. I rolled up my school skirt to make it shorter and applied a bit of lipstick, then undid it all when I came home. Mum still told me off. It must have been Joyce across the road, or maybe Mavis, who reported to Mum whenever I was late.

As kids, we couldn't get away with anything. And, boy, did we try. In all honesty I was just trying to fit in. I couldn't wear designer clothes or the latest trainers, but I could make myself cool wearing make-up and short skirts.

Mum used to say things like 'Sticks and stones may break your bones, but words can never hurt you,' as she packed me out of the door when I was upset about something. She was often matter of fact and never handled us with kid gloves. This, I later learned, was her way of preparing me for and trying to protect me against the racism and abuse I would inevitably suffer in later life. But when I was around fourteen, she once stressed to me how special I was. I must have been feeling particularly low that day, when suddenly she said, 'I almost lost you . . . You were a twin and your twin died and the doctors thought I would lose you too.' Mum never shared personal details like that – West Indian parents can be very secretive – so I was shocked. It made me stop to think. It's one of life's miracles that we're on this planet in the first place, so to know that I'm a surviving twin made me feel I was here for a purpose. A bigger purpose than I could ever imagine. If I'm honest with myself, I don't feel I've ful-filled it yet. The best is still to come. I really wish that my twin had survived because I think we would have been formidable – world domination for sure. When I get car-ried away, I occasionally wonder how the world would have coped with two Dawn Butlers!

My mum used to tell me to ignore people who said horrible things about me because I had a bigger purpose. Resilience in action. Mum and Dad had been resilient when they came to England because they were fighting so many fires. They couldn't take offence at every racist or ignorant comment or they wouldn't have been able to get through the day or find any joy in their lives. During the Covid pandemic, my mum and I were walking along Leytonstone High Road when she pointed to a street cor-ner. She mentioned that as she had pushed my brothers in a pram past that spot, a woman had come out every morning with her dog just to make sure it barked at them. It was the first time my mum had told me this story, and I was awed by how much racism she had put up with in those days. My mum clenched her fist. She'd soon had enough. The next time she left the house, she took a stick with her, ready to defend herself and our family. Mum said, 'That was the last time she did it.'

Recalling my parents' stories reminds me of why the Windrush scandal of 2017 felt so cruel. People like my par-ents, who have been through so much, were basically told they were old and surplus to requirements. They were denied basic rights and healthcare, lost their homes and jobs, were forced into debt, and even wrongly deported, separated from their families. What a grave injustice and betrayal, given that the Windrush generation were invited to this country to help rebuild it after the war, and have contributed so much to society. Many of my constituents had nothing left to give to this fight, their resilience worn down. This generation, previously full of pride, was too embarrassed to tell their children and grandchildren what was happening. The shame they felt, as though they had done something wrong, is a classic reaction from people who have had the fight taken out of them. It took an ally, a white journalist named Amelia Gentleman, to expose the injustice and get people listening.

My parents always wanted a relatively quiet life. Most people do. They sacrificed a lot and took abuse, not only to survive the day but to make other people feel comfortable. They had had to build a steady resilience. For me, things are different. Activism, speaking up, speaking out, voicing my opinions and experiences has always been very important to me, despite all the baggage and the bullying that comes with it. I don't just want to survive; I want to strive and build a better world for those coming behind me. My parents' generation have brought us this far. It's up to us now to lead the revolution.

*

When it comes down to it, I was definitely a daddy's girl, so whatever he did, I did. If he was under the bonnet of a car, I was too, learning how to fix it. I worked with my dad from when I was around thirteen at what eventually became the family-owned West Indian bakery on Selby Road, Leytonstone. Sometimes I woke at 3 a.m. to work with him, learning how to knead and mould bread by hand. At that age, I could handle the oven (I still have the burn marks on my arm), put bread in and take it out – a particular skill. I liked scoring the top of the loaves (so they don't burst). After a few hours doing that I went to school, only to come back to the bakery later. I always had to be doing something, whether it was running a homework club at the back of my dad's van or selling lemonade and flowers. (I cut them from someone else's garden and that business model didn't last long: I was caught!) Regardless, I would say that I was an awesome kid, although my teachers would probably have had a different view.

I have no idea what inspired my dad to buy the bakery. All I know is that he often baked with my uncles, Buck and Gillie, and it seemed to be another string to add to his bow. He ran the bakery like a soup kitchen and never seemed to be bothered about making a profit. We survived by working for free as a family to keep the place going. If someone came in hungry, my dad made sure they had something to eat – he never gave someone a stale roll just because they couldn't afford it: they received a fresh roll straight from the oven. He wanted people to have something nice to eat, not to feel grateful for leftovers. This, in a way, inspired my socialist principles.

There is a famous saying from the fight for women's rights: 'We want bread, but we want roses too!' A testament to ensuring people have dignity in their lives. Whether my dad was supplying West Indian bread for funerals or other functions, it was never a problem or a chore, and he never wanted credit for it.

Our customers didn't come to Butlers Bakery just to be served. They lingered to have conversations, creating a real sense of community that I think is lacking today. If you know anything about West Indian shops and their reputation for providing poor customer service, then you know how unique this was. Speak to anyone who visited our shop and they will have a fond memory to tell you. The bakery helped me to perfect speaking with people from all walks of life, and when it closed at 6 p.m., customers stuck around to continue chatting, turning the place into a debating forum until we were tired and had to usher everyone out.

The bakery was a hive of activity, a place where people came to put the world to rights, and what I learned there was different from anything I could have been taught in school. I observed differing points of view, and sometimes discussions were heated. But I saw people would leave the shop knowing they had gained some knowledge or understanding from the debate, even if they didn't agree with everything that had been said. Everyone was heard and listened to, not dismissed, or ignored, and every voice was seen as valuable. This is what happens in strong communities. There wasn't an expectation of everyone having the same world view, and all ideas and thoughts were welcome. You could agree to disagree, and still come away having learned something new. That openness and willingness to hear and process an alternative point of view is crucial, especially these days, when divisions are constantly sown in the media or in government between Us and Them.

My time at the bakery also impressed upon me the power of teamwork, of the necessity for people to come together around a common goal. My dad employed this young girl, Pat, to work with me on a Saturday. I was initially reluctant to have a new colleague: I didn't want to have to show her the ropes or have her hang around me but, unknown to me, he'd hatched this plan with her parents. They felt I would be a good influence on her, and that working at the bakery would give her beneficial life skills. I still think about how better to implement this in a city like London, especially during such unstable times. We should have more mentoring, and more paid work experience, building the confidence of the next generation.

There were two bakers at the shop: my dad and Cousin Arthur – if Arthur didn't turn up for a shift, my dad could manage the whole operation himself. He could always use an extra pair of hands, though, so he used to get someone to fill in, even if they were a non-baker. They most likely didn't have all the skills required, but my dad liked to get a rhythm going with someone who could fulfil a specific role. Looking back, these were my introductions to learning how to delegate, communicate, and ask for help when needed. I would see the stand-in bakers having to think outside the box, using whatever skills they had.

Everyone has their own gifts that can contribute to a whole. There is no such thing as unskilled work, as anyone who has had trouble scanning their shopping can testify. Being in that environment as a young teenager taught me the importance of having good people around you, and instilled in me respect for knowledge, information and skill. I will never forget one piece of advice in particular. A pastry chef who worked with us told me: 'Follow the recipe the first time. It's written in that way for a reason,' he said, and although I might like something a bit sweeter, I should follow it carefully the first time to understand why it had been created as it was. Once I understood that, it was easier to change it. As someone anxious to dismantle many of the systems we operate within, or at least see them evolve and change in meaningful ways, I have found this useful advice.

While my eldest sister Sharon baked the cakes, it was my job to decorate them, and to enhance the few skills I had, I thought I should enrol in Waltham Forest College for a cake-decorating course. I only went to the first class. Instead of going to the others, I spent time with my mates, Kelly and Michelle, having a laugh and eating kebabs. That was great until one day someone ordered a highly decorated cake. I did such a horrible job I had to give them the cake for free and their deposit back too, in the hope that they wouldn't complain.

After that, I started attending classes. Well, most of them. Once I got the gist, I skipped a few. There are some things in life you just can't fake, and complex cake decorating is one of them.

Butlers Bakery no longer exists. My family stopped running it after my dad passed away in 2011. On the day of his funeral, people had lined up outside the bakery and all along the road to pay their respects as my family passed on the way to the service. Once we got to the 500-seat church, there was not enough room to accommodate everyone, and people were standing inside and out. So many people loved him, and for good reason.

Now, the bakery is an official community café, and I am proud to say that in 2021 I was honoured with a blue plaque by Waltham Forest Heritage after residents nominated me as a local hero. But the honour really belongs to the memory of my dad and his legacy. When the shop officially closed, some of our oldest customers were in tears, with one woman telling me that it had been the highlight of her day. Hearing her speak about coming in for a chat with my mum reminded me of how we cannot take for granted the power of connection and building bonds. Human beings were not built for isolation, but to share and communicate with each other.

I witnessed people grow from child to adult at the bakery, and I have memories and friends for life through that connection. Pat and I witnessed the journey of our customers from buying a jam doughnut to West Indian hardo bread. The sign of a proper adult. Some of our customers are well-known now, names such as Dalton Grant, Ben Ofoedu and the very famous actor and DJ Idris Elba. The stories I could tell would fill another book.

When I was eight, my neighbourhood came together for a street party in celebration of the Queen during the Silver Jubilee. We were all outside, tables set up along the road with plates of egg sandwiches, and colourful decorations. Our street felt safe – our street *was* safe. People looked out for each other. That kind of togetherness set the stage for a way of life that became completely normal for me – people of all backgrounds and ethnicities mucking in and getting along. When Margaret Thatcher said, 'There's no such thing as society,' it made no sense to me: I was lucky enough to be born into a family and community that helped and supported each other. My upbringing in Leytonstone taught me the value of diversity and community spirit, and these are the attributes that are the best of what London has to offer.

Political erosion of society has been a failed Tory experiment, something we became more aware of during the coronavirus pandemic. They continually try to get people looking the other way while they pickpocket you of your rights and compassion. Margaret Thatcher would not have tried so hard to dismantle our communities, let alone our trade unions, if they had not been so strong. There is a well-known saying, 'United we stand. Divided we fall.' This was the model Thatcher was trying to break. The idea of simply looking after yourself to the degree that you become self-serving has destroyed the fabric of our society. This is why, at this critical juncture in time, it is important to band together, to believe in the power of the people, and to reject the agendas of division and hate that are being sown. We are all human beings and the one thing we all have in common is that we are born and one day we will die.

A few years ago, when one of my childhood neighbours, Mr Harris, died, all of us adults who had known each other as kids gathered for his funeral. We had a shared history that no one could understand and a bond that would never be broken. When we shared our stories we laughed: nobody but us could understand or even believe how much we got up to as neighbours. I thought that kind of unity would be the world I would navigate as an adult, a melting pot of people and cultures, but I would soon be proven wrong.

In London, and most likely across Britain, our small shops and community centres are disappearing, either bought up by developers or abandoned because the rents are unaffordable. Crucial social connections are not made, and the community spirit that I believe is the missing link to tackling many of the social issues we are facing in modern society disappears. I want to bring London back to that place for the young people who have never experienced this type of Butlers Bakery unity in their community. I feel my purpose is to recreate it, and I do not think it an impossible dream.

There have been moments in more recent years when

we have all had to pull together, like the 2012 Olympics. For two wonderful weeks in London, people opened up, said hello to each other on the trains – the atmosphere felt happy and welcoming – and when the Games ended, it was back to business as usual. Overnight, people seemed to return to reading their papers and mobile phones. Then in 2020 we were faced with the terrible crisis of the pandemic. Despite the incredible difficulties that each of us encountered, we saw communities come together to support each other.

New challenges were brought to me, as the MP for Brent Central, each day, whether they were from constituents stranded in different countries and trying to make their way home, or someone who was fighting with her mother's funeral insurance. Of course, not all of her mum's plans could be implemented, given the circumstances, but dressing her in her favourite outfit should have been possible. The family were distraught, in tears, and so was I. 'We last saw her going into an ambulance,' they said to me. I contacted the funeral directors and, after some strong words, the family got to say a proper goodbye.

My emotions were running high, and in the face of such challenges I needed to balance the pressure of my days by doing something active. Otherwise I was going to have a full-blown meltdown. I got involved with packing and delivering food parcels in Brent, making sure the most vulnerable were fed. There was a central packing point, Bridge Park, where businesses donated the basics, like bread, pasta and beans. We put these items in boxes and took them to people on the council's shielding list. For me, it felt nice to get out of the house, to interact and connect with others, and to participate in a common goal or task. A bit like being in the bakery all those years ago – there's something gratifying about being of service and teamwork.

Everything came to a halt during the pandemic, which gave us time to consider the people around us, not just our families and friends, but our neighbours too. For many people, it might have been the first time neighbours checked in on each other. I know my own neighbours well, but I got to know many more households around me during lockdown as I made my rounds as the MP. It was great because more people were at home for me to check on, making sure they were okay. People talked about how they were able to acknowledge each other now and make more of an effort to say hello instead of coming home from work and disappearing inside.

This unity required us to come out of our comfort zones and trust each other a little bit more so that we could form stronger connections. The pandemic made us all feel closer to each other, and the threat of illness made us care about those we might not have thought too much about before. The simple act of saying hello makes you feel more invested in a person, and now people were saying things like 'Have you seen Chris? I haven't seen him in a few days.' These connections make you feel part of where you live, allowing you to take interest in the lives of others as well as your own. This is also why we need to tackle the rental crisis, and fight for more affordable housing and better mortgage agreements, so that people can buy their homes and put down roots.

Forging meaningful relationships with those outside our immediate horizons can start with where you work or live, but it requires you to pay attention to your colleagues or neighbours, or even the people you might see every day at the shops or on the train but hardly interact with. How do we make more of an effort to connect with each other? We step out of our comfort zones and temporarily set aside our own preoccupations and preconceptions. We get curious, ask questions, and actively listen to others. For us Londoners, it can be daunting. When we go up north, we can be taken aback by how helpful people are, especially when giving directions. But it starts with a simple smile, then a hello.

If you're stuck for something to say, try a compliment: *I like your outfit/your hair/your coat*, basically anything nice. This interaction can be fun to weave into your day. It doesn't mean you're going to be friends with everyone you're nice to. You're just making society warmer, friendlier. The other day a woman apologetically pushed me on the train as she tried to squeeze in at the last minute, and I smiled warmly at her. Although I had my mask on, she could see the smile in my eyes and she smiled back. When two seats became available, I rushed, as you do on a crowded train, to be the first to sit down. Then I noticed she was right behind me, so I offered her the seat closest to me and took the other so we could both be sure of getting one. We laughed. We never spoke, but we made each other laugh.

We can build on conversations so that all involved feel seen and heard. Community will mean something different to everyone but these practices can happen at the shops, in our neighbourhoods, our gyms, our places of worship or wherever we might volunteer.

Post-pandemic, things have returned mostly to normal, but I'm still wondering how we can continue to replicate that tightness, that togetherness without a crisis. In times of need, community is a safety net, an extra support and comfort, and I believe we need to make our communities stronger, especially when so much is eroding before our eyes.

2

A GOOD TEACHER MAKES
ALL THE DIFFERENCE

AS A SCHOOLKID, I WAS FEARLESS. Nothing fazed me. Well, nothing but those flying cockroaches, and going to the dentist. Mum told my brothers to take me to the surgery just around the corner, and they enjoyed sharing with me how the dentist would hang my teeth on the long metal stand I could see from the practice window. They started laughing, but I was scared and ran away to hide under a car until it was dark, and the dentist shut their doors. Then and there I swore never to need a dentist, and had my first and only filling at the age of forty-five.

My brothers didn't just tease me, though. My parents may have taught me resilience – 'Sticks and stones . . .' – but my three older brothers taught me resistance. From quite an early age they taught me how to fight and defend myself with words: they didn't want me to let injustices go. They said that the names others call you can have a psychological effect on how you see yourself and process information. They implored me not to accept abuse or allow myself to be belittled. If you can stand firm in your centre, in your purpose and in your truth, the next person following doesn't have to suffer.

Occasionally we had fist fights in school. When the show *Roots* was on TV in the late seventies my white classmates started calling us Black kids 'Kunta Kinte' (the enslaved character) and saying we should all be whipped. We were not going to stand for that. It was also not uncommon for brawls to erupt between schools on a Friday afternoon – I only ever remember my school winning, but apparently, according to an old 'enemy', we supposedly lost some fights too! As a unit, we stuck together against what we perceived to be common rivals, but internally we had our own problems (a pattern you might recognize in politics, too). In Jennifer Eberhardt's book *Biased*, she refers to the power of context to weaken bias.[1] Faced with a common enemy, research has shown that our biases can be temporarily dissolved by the urge to band together to survive.

Growing up alongside my four brothers and sister, I was forced to be bold and to speak up or no one took me seriously. When my siblings teased me, I had to learn to defend myself, but even though I was the prime target, I knew at the end of it all that they loved me and would always have my back. No one could harm me because my older brothers would be there for me in an instant. They stressed from an early age that if I was ever in trouble I should find them or get a message to them – difficult in a world without mobile phones. But having that safety net triggered confidence within me. I'm sure my teachers were unable to handle me because of it. I was determined, passionate and caring, but talkative and easily bored, too. I asserted myself in school so that nobody troubled me, and it also meant nobody troubled my friends.

The need to question and challenge, and to fight for what is right, has always been a part of who I am. At an early age I found myself disagreeing with some of my teachers' decision-making. A classmate was being bullied repeatedly by the same kid, and the teacher did nothing to stop it. When my classmate finally lashed out at the bully, the teacher wanted to send them outside the classroom door, but I stood up and protested: why was my classmate being punished for defending themselves, especially when the teacher had failed to protect them?

Or take sports day. We used to get bus tickets to go to Drapers Field, a playing field in East London, about a mile away from school. One winter's day when I was probably around eleven, I declared it was too cold to be running around the field in nylon pants and top, which was the customary sports kit. In the hall I organized a sit-in, and the other kids, convinced by my arguments, decided to join me. The teachers couldn't get us to run that day. They were all fuming, and after about an hour, they acquiesced but punished the lot of us by making us walk back to school instead of taking the bus. My old primary-school friend, Brenda, still cusses me to this day for my stupid strike, but at the time I was quite pleased with myself. And, as I told her, at least we were fully dressed when we walked back.

There came a point in my education when I thought, *School isn't for me*. I felt misunderstood by my teachers. I used to tear out pages from my report book because the comments were so bad, and I didn't want get into trouble if my parents read them. Unfortunately, my teachers had formed an image of me, and I couldn't help but think this was affecting how they graded me. Yes, I was outspoken, and I often questioned everything, and this got on my teachers' nerves, but how else was I to learn?

I had an inquisitive nature. At Bible study class, I was thrown out for being too much trouble: I had questioned the role of women. 'Why was Eve punished with periods for forcing Adam to eat an apple?' I would ask. But so much that I was taught didn't make sense and it seemed ridiculous that I wasn't supposed to ask questions. In school I would ask why there was a way to tell the relationship status of a woman, Miss or Mrs, but only Mr for a man.

When I suspected some of the grades I received might be due to my teachers' biases, I put my theory to the test in the history class. I couldn't ask my teachers outright about their grading system, which would have been too confrontational, so I took another route. I had a white friend named Andrea who was a straight-A student. We used to have competitions to see who could write the neatest and the smallest: our handwriting was almost identical.

I asked her one day if we could swap our homework, and when the grades came the next day, she still got an A. I received a C or a D. 'See?' I said to her. 'This is what I mean!' The proof was in front of our eyes, and I wanted to do something with the evidence, but I could tell that Andrea was terrified because she asked me not to tell anyone. 'No!' I cried. 'We've got to! I want my A – that's my A. I deserve that A.' In the end, I kept my mouth shut because I didn't want to get Andrea into trouble.

After that episode, I simply thought, *I've really had enough of school this time*. I couldn't drop out, my parents would never have let me, so instead I mentally checked out.

If it hadn't been for my computer teacher, Mr Taylor, who took an interest in teaching me, things would probably have turned out somewhat differently. I've talked about Mr Taylor several times throughout my career and often during school visits. I have tried to search for him over the years, but have not been able to find him. I remember him as a tall white guy with dark curly hair, who saw that I had a brain and that it worked in a particular way. If there was a problem, I had to find a solution to it, no matter what it was. I learn by questioning, by investigating the possibilities, and he thought that I should apply that drive to computing and coding. Mr Taylor didn't have a preconceived idea about me, and he didn't allow staffroom chatter to cloud his view. He saw my capabilities and his kind, patient commitment to me made me more determined to do well. I like to imagine that maybe, just maybe, he changed the chatter in the staffroom as my grades began to improve. He also set me on my career path in computing. Sometimes you need only one person to be your ally for things to change.

Awareness that many systems, like policing and health, are structurally flawed strikes me time and time again. We are living in a time where the cracks are more than starting to show, and it is interesting to reflect on my schooling and to think about how the system still repeatedly fails Black Caribbean children some forty years on. In 2021, the *Guardian* published an article stating that 'Exclusion rates for Black Caribbean students in English schools are up to six times higher than those of their white peers in some local authorities,'[2] with 'Gypsy, Roma and Traveller children' also deeply affected. Not every child learns in the same way, which is something I can definitely relate to, and this statistic illustrates just how rigid our school systems can be. It also highlights how unconscious bias comes into play across class, race and ethnicity, which has damaging and long-lasting effects on Black children. In 2020, a YMCA report wrote that 'half of young Black people (50%) believe that teachers' perceptions of them are one of the biggest barriers to their achievement in school'.[3]

This reminds me of what my brothers pointed out to me so long ago, about resisting other people labelling you, and sometimes that includes teachers. If Black children believe they are troublesome or incapable of learning, the stigma follows them around and seeps into their consciousness. But often it is a failing of a rigid school system that is unwilling to accommodate differing learning needs or unable to experiment with more wide-ranging teaching techniques.

An unsatisfactory teacher overpowers and dominates their students, corrupting the system beyond measure. It is upsetting to think that young people today are still battling what I went through all those years ago with many of my own teachers. A good teacher makes all the difference, and if it wasn't for Mr Taylor, my life would probably have taken a different turn. So many youths in London don't experience this positive intervention, as evidenced in the school-to-prison pipeline. Children who are excluded or suspended from school have a higher chance of going to prison: their early experiences of excessive punishment and disciplinary actions criminalize them.

If we want to address some of the issues around crime, for example, we must investigate why kids are being excluded and treat them with as much care as we do those who can successfully navigate the system. If teachers and schools are treating young children as vexing and punishing them, instead of handling them with attention and consideration, there will be negative outcomes. We must look at what lies behind these children's actions, whether it's trauma, behavioural issues, or different ways of learning, and equip teachers with the skills to address these issues within their classrooms. We also need mental-health specialists attached to every school.

We need to reinvent pupil referral units (PRUs): now,

essentially, we are placing kids in a system that almost guarantees they will encounter a poor education, criminality and perhaps even a prison sentence. We should look at how we can staff PRUs so that they become a hub of hope, rehabilitation, education and learning, not just a place where society dumps 'troublesome' kids and abandons them. Understanding that we need to treat disturbance from children as a mental-health not a criminal issue is essential to breaking the cycle. It is in all our interests to ensure that we have well-educated and well-rounded children. An African proverb says 'It takes a village to raise a child.' We should all play our role in that village, and being aware of the root of the problem is the first step.

Once we understand that not all kids learn by chalk and talk, basically being lectured at, we realize we are overlooking some potentially talented kids in the classroom. PRUs are not where the best educators are to be found but they should be. Often the kids who are not paying attention are super-bright, but some may have behavioural or special-needs issues that require additional time and attention. If we invested in the quality of teaching, and helping kids to understand who they are, alongside how to debate and how to resolve conflict, if we keep them busy and interested in subjects and activities that appeal to them, they are less likely to be enticed into crime or the destructive behaviour that is so often programmed into their psyche from early experiences of exclusion and punishment. This is where the power of community comes back into play.

As I said earlier, I was taught my most important lessons outside the classroom, in the bakery, where I not only learned from my dad and the other adults around me, like the pastry chef, but also from the customers who came in to debate. If kids cannot thrive in school, if they are not surrounded there by people who take the time to understand them and their needs, perhaps others in the community have the time and the willingness to teach them and foster in them a sense of self-worth and self-confidence, as well as a learned skill that can help them in the future. This is why community centres, small, independent shops and Saturday schools – where great authors like Akala, who has written extensively on the barriers of race, class and privilege, were educated – are so important. We need places where generations can potentially mix and where young people can learn skills and vocations outside school.

I cannot claim to have all the answers to how our school system should change. All I know is that it starts with our teachers, or our governing bodies, and that adequate training or continual training needs to be put in place so that those who are responsible for our kids treat all of them with the patience and dignity they deserve. Once people understand how bias works they become better educators. As a Black child growing up and being taught by teachers who did not understand me or my needs and were often blinded by their biases, it was essential that someone like Mr Taylor intervene to show me how to target the skills I had. I know I am not alone. In his book

Natives, Akala stresses that some of his white middle-class teachers made his school life extremely difficult and penalized him for the very thing they should have been nurturing: his intelligence. Mr Taylor could look beyond the one-dimensional image so many teachers have of Black kids, a skill the teacher who called me a liar at eight years old was unable to grasp. Because she had never seen a flying cockroach, she wanted to confine me to her own limitations instead of recognizing that I had something to teach her, based on my experience and cultural background.

Although I am no longer eight, the battle is still the same. Throughout my career as an MP, I have been accused of lying, of speaking too much or too long, and of basically taking up too much space. At every turn people try to stop me or shut me up. But I will not allow others to dim my light, ignore my achievements or call me a liar when I'm telling the truth.

3

DRIVING WHILE BLACK

To talk about my youth without mentioning the police would give an incomplete story. If you know me and my work, you'll know how passionate I am about police reform despite the abuse it often attracts to me. It was my brothers who talked to me about the police when I was about thirteen. They told me never to be alone with an officer, and that I should contact them if ever something happened to me. They also told me, before I even thought about driving, to look into my rear-view mirror whenever I saw a police car driving past. This was to see if the car would turn to follow me.

When I finally got my licence, I drove everywhere, and was often the designated driver for my friends. I had a convertible, so if it was sunny Pat would call me, even after a night of raving and a hard morning's work at the bakery, to ensure we had a fun day planned.

When I was eighteen, I was at a party a five-minute drive from my house. An argument erupted outside when the next-door neighbour, a white male, got angry about the noise. Things escalated quickly, and the man threw a brick at my car window. Someone ran in to tell me, and when I came out, my window was smashed. I shouted at the guy, angry at the damage he'd caused, and asked him what he'd thought he was doing. In response, he went back into his house and came out again with a knife. I said to Pat, 'Quick! Go and get my brothers.'

When Owen arrived on the scene, he tried to ask what was going on but the man lunged at him with the knife and tried to stab him. There was a lot of yelling, and by this point, I decided to call the police. I thought, *If I don't do it now, this guy's going to kill my brother.*

The police arrived in a van, but instead of arresting the guy, who still had the knife in his hand, they came for my brother. I remember screaming, saying that my brother was innocent and had only come to help me. I couldn't understand why he was being thrown into the van, when the other guy was still holding the weapon. They would later arrest the white man, but it would be too late in terms of the mental and physical scars that my brother gained from the experience.

At eighteen, I was so outraged that I wrote a formal letter of complaint to the police. When I received an official letter of apology, I was pleased with myself, naively believing this was progress. My teenage self saw the piece of paper in my hand as a victory, so much so that I ran to show my brother. 'Look, bro, we got a letter of apology from the police!' But all these years later, as a grown woman, I realize that letter was nowhere near enough. A letter of apology holds no one to account. It doesn't change a structure, or make people examine their internalized biases, or dismantle a racist police system. It's simply words on a page meant to placate the recipient in that moment. It doesn't ensure that the same sort of behaviour won't happen again to another Black family asking for help. Years later, and many official reports later, the police have been found to be institutionally racist, sexist, homophobic, misogynistic and corrupt.

When I first heard about the George Floyd video in 2021, my mind immediately went to that incident more than three decades earlier. I called my brother. 'Do you remember when the police arrested you? When the white guy tried to stab you with a knife?'

My brother's response was simple and to the point: 'Do I remember, sis? I've still got the scars.' When they put him in the van, the police pinned him to the floor, their knees on his neck and back. To this day he's got a scar on his wrist where they put handcuffs on him, drawing blood. As he shared the details of that day, I realized that things could have escalated: I could have lost my brother because he came to help me. Tears fell down my face as he spoke. *I could have lost him*, I thought, *and it would have been my fault because I'd called the police*.

It is difficult for me to explain to those who have only ever felt protected by the police the generational trauma that exists within the Black community, but everyone has their own traumatic story to tell. My brother Donald was badly beaten up by a gang of racists after school, my brother Tennyson was mugged for his trainers and my other brother John was almost killed by his own colleagues when he was serving in the army. When people went out to protest during Black Lives Matter after the death of George Floyd, they weren't just marching for that moment. They were fighting for structural and systemic change, and they hoped that if the Black community was listened to and believed, rather than being accused of lying or exaggerating, police forces and other institutions around the world could rid themselves of very dangerous individuals. People were protesting so that things changed permanently, so that police services began to examine their internalized biases against Black men as aggressors, threats and criminals. You won't always be able to change individuals, but if you can change the system so that it works to punish bad behaviour, that's progress. It was Martin Luther King who said, 'It may be true that the law cannot make a man love me, but it can stop him from lynching me, and I think that's pretty important.'[1]

There's been a lot of talk about the problems in the police service with many people saying it's just a few bad apples, but to deny that the police are institutionally racist, sexist and homophobic only guarantees that unjust and often life-threatening behaviour goes unchecked. Our systems are in desperate need of an overhaul to ensure accountability and fairness. I know there are many good officers and, as an MP, I have a very good relationship with my local police. We work well together to tackle current issues, and we try to build community trust. But it took work.

We all have prejudices and biases, and my own experiences of the police made me cautious. When I became a newly elected MP, I undertook some outreach work, deciding I would go out late at night with a youth community leadership group to engage with young people on the streets. We were in the Stonebridge Estate, which no longer exists, and as we were chatting, the police came screeching up in their cars, flashing their blues and twos. Some young people ran, others dropped their bikes and disappeared. I ran too: it was my muscle memory of previous encounters. As I turned the corner and noticed that my staff member wasn't with me, I checked myself, reminding myself that I didn't need to run. I was the MP. I took a deep breath, turned back, stretched out my hand and said, 'Good evening, officer. My name is Dawn Butler, and I am the MP for Brent.' I don't think he believed me at first, but I stood firm and questioned his approach – screeching up to us had been very scary. We had a conversation and then he left.

The young people were impressed with me – I definitely got some street cred that day, but they obviously hadn't seen me running! But as I said to them, 'If you have nothing to hide, you shouldn't need to run.' I believe that, but with policing it sadly isn't that simple. Why take the risk of encountering a 'bad apple' racist cop, when you can just run away and escape that trauma?

Good policing is local policing, and that is true in the UK, America or anywhere else in the world. Local policing understands the community it serves and polices accordingly. To solve crime, you need to build up a rapport with the community. The problem is that local policing isn't much valued in the current system. As I have got to understand how policing works, I have been told by officers that the more people you arrest or the more people you stop and search, the more the system recognizes you as a better officer, even if your success rate is very poor. By this measure, the more often you take these wrong ineffective actions, the faster you can progress in your career: no credit is given to good policing, just numbers. In my experience, the most valuable police officers are not those who have made the most arrests. The local police who really know the community they're serving have a greater impact.

The current approach is a classic case of structural racism. It's strange that the police force rewards officers who, say, stop and search a hundred people a week: this intervention has a success rate of between 11 and 13 per cent when it comes to finding any criminal activity leading to arrest.[2] In what other job is a person rewarded for such a low success rate? And in what other job would such an unsuccessful strategy continue to be used? Policing needs to be intelligence-led. The structural problem of the police rewarding bad behaviour and practices is why we have so many poor and unnecessary stop-and-searches. Rather than relying on intelligence gathered by local policing and making a targeted approach, stop-and-search measures reinforce the view that everyone stopped might be implicated in a crime. And the claim that more Black boys commit crime than other demographics is just an excuse to keep a rotten racist structure going.

What some people fail to understand about stop-and-search is that every time it happens to a young Black boy or man, it takes away their liberty, and it can have an impact on their self-esteem or affect their mental health. Constant surveillance and scrutiny take place from a very early age, which makes them feel they're not allowed to go about their business because they're Black. It's not difficult to imagine the mental-health issues that are brought on by the trauma of being racialized and profiled regularly, not to mention the distrust of authorities. It's a heartbreaking invasion and diminishment of self-worth.

The disproportionate enforcement of certain policies such as stop-and-search, whether on the ground or in vehicles, and the use of handcuffs pre-arrest, builds up resentment. It can also, at times, create hatred of one's own skin colour, making it easier for young Black boys to attack others who look like them because they don't see themselves reflected in a positive enough light. Recently, I wore a luminous orange jacket to a speaking event, and someone said, 'Well, you can't be missed in that. You'd better be careful you don't get arrested.' If every time they walked out of their house with that jacket on and were stopped and questioned by police, or even arrested, I asked, how would they feel about the jacket? Would they begin to hate it because of the problems it caused? I questioned whether they would want to leave the jacket at home in future.

I'm grateful that my dad was such an encouraging

influence on my brothers, that he was there to teach them to love themselves, despite outside forces chipping away at their self-worth. They also had the support of each other and our wider family network. But not everybody has that support. If we want to create a safer and better society, we must recreate the support structure in our schools, institutions and communities.

One of my goals as the MP for Brent Central has always been to reduce violence. I know this can be done if we take a holistic approach to the problem, hence my belief in local policing. Local officers can tell you who the criminals really are because they have local intelligence and expertise, meaning you don't have to rely on ineffective, discriminatory measures. The community gets together to fix the problem because they care and don't want criminal activity in their area.

*

My first stop by the police happened when I was in my early twenties. I was driving about two miles to the bakery early one morning when a police car passed me. I remembered the advice my brothers had given me when I was younger so I looked in my rear-view mirror. Sure enough the police had U-turned and were following me. My brothers had told me that if I was being followed I should stop in a place where I knew I'd be protected. The police wanted to pull me over but the roads were empty: I was only a few minutes away from the bakery and wanted to stop in a place that felt safe. When I arrived, I parked the car.

The police approached me, told me to get out, and were shocked to see that I was female. They must have presumed I was a Black male in a convertible car – because of the cold, I was wearing a hat and a bulky jacket. They asked me a question or two, which I answered, and then they said, 'You can get into your car and be on your way.'

And to this I replied, 'No, *you* can get in your car and be on *your* way because I've reached my destination.' I felt emboldened to say that because I was in a safe space and knew they had nothing on me – and they knew that too. I had arrived at my destination and felt confident. There's something to be said about being comfortable on your own turf rather than vulnerable in unfamiliar surroundings.

Fast forward some three decades, with a few more stops in between. I was committed to changing structural issues within the police, so much so that on 8 August 2020 I wrote an honest, hard-hitting article for the *Metro* titled 'Black people should not be scared to phone the police when they need help – but I was', which called for the commissioner at the time, Cressida Dick, to resign. I stated that:

> At this most pivotal time the commissioner thought it appropriate to say that 'institutionally racist' is not a 'useful way to describe' the force, which is not only unhelpful but offensive. It is quite telling.
>
> Cressida Dick appears to be incapable of tackling this long-known problem, and incapable of showing

solidarity with those people who suffer from it the most, so she should resign.

It is not something I call for easily. I know too that the word racist often scares people, but it does not mean every officer is racist – nor am I calling Cressida Dick racist. It's the Met Police organization that is structurally racist and she is in charge of it. We need her to tackle it, not deny our lived experiences or make excuses.

I know that the Met contains a lot of good, brave people, including hardworking officers here in Brent whom I work with closely. They risk their lives to protect the public, so I know these good officers won't want the bad ones, or a racist system, giving them a bad name. Positive change will be for the benefit of us all.[3]

Just a day after that article's publication on 9 August 2020, a friend of mine and I were dramatically stopped by the police in Hackney. I recorded the incident and posted it online, and I am still getting unfair abuse, and being called a liar on social media to this day (especially from people who claim to be police officers, serving and former). It has taken two years to piece together most of the puzzle of what happened that day and I am now able to tell the story in full.

My friend and I were headed out for lunch. It was a rare treat, as I had the day off and it was a perfect sunny Sunday afternoon. A marked police car with its blues and twos drove past us as we slowly approached the traffic lights. I thought the officers were rushing to an emergency call and I said to my friend, 'Oh, I hope every-thing's okay.' As an MP I always worry about these things. We watched the police car U-turn and the next thing I knew there were lights flashing behind us. It was another police car, so I said to my friend, 'Move over. Let the police car through. There must be a big emergency.'

He looked at me, laughed at my concern, and said, 'They're stopping us.' I was so confused, and couldn't understand why. We were having a great day in the sun, and the police car in front would have seen us chatting and smiling, so why pull us over? It transpired that we were basically the filling in a cop-car sandwich.

An officer approached my friend. He said he needed to run a few checks, leaned in and removed my friend's keys. My friend was completely compliant and even handed over his driving licence without being asked for it. A sign of someone resigned to being stopped. Just that week I'd had a disagreement with the then commissioner, Cressida Dick, about how Black people are dispropor-tionately stopped, so I started recording the incident. Another young police officer approached me at the pas-senger side and started to question me, asking where we were going. I told him we were going out, and basically the rest was none of his business. He proceeded to ask me if I lived in London. Bemused, I asked him what the relevance was of his questioning. Now remember, good policing should be intelligence-led. The young offi-cer told me that they were doing protective patrols in

Hackney combating gang and knife crime, and they also needed to know that people were driving legitimately. My friend and I did not exactly fit the profile of a gang, unless they were basing it on our skin colour. Only now, months later, I wonder if I was being taught a lesson: after all, I'd called for the resignation of the commissioner just twenty-four hours earlier.

The police officer came back to the driver's side and said that when he had put the number plate into the system it came up as being registered in North Yorkshire, but when he ran it through a second time there were no issues. He clearly thought that would be the end of it, but I am not eighteen any more: I needed to know what had gone wrong and why. I asked if the system was wrong, and the officer replied, 'Yes.' He said he had typed in the registration number and it came up with the same make, model and colour of our vehicle, but that it was registered in North Yorkshire.

'How is that possible?' I asked. I needed to know so that I could help my constituents and anyone else who was stopped in the future. The officer was polite enough but unable to explain the discrepancy.

It was only then that I identified myself. I wanted the officer to know that getting to the root of the problem was important for me and my research as an MP. The officer shifted a little, apologized, and said that the police get a lot of people who aren't registered locally so they needed to do a few checks.

Woah, I thought. *Hang on a minute. You're not allowed*

to drive in Hackney unless you live there? When did that become a rule? I probed further. Remember, the act of depriving someone of their liberty should not be taken lightly.

I asked the officer if he thought we were running county lines, which is the act of supplying drugs into neighbouring counties. He gave a muddle of reasons as to why we had been stopped and none of them made sense. Was it a drug stop or a traffic stop? And why us? This wasn't intelligence-led policing. It was as simple as that. This stop stank and I wasn't about to accept an apology, as I had done when I was younger, because that wouldn't change the system. I told the officer that I was concerned about the reason for the stop. And I calmly explained that profiling people because of the colour of their skin or because they are driving a certain type of car is inappropriate.

A third officer decided to approach us, obviously thinking she could shut us down. 'You can't see into the car because of the tints at the back,' she said. She tried to argue that, because they couldn't see into the car, anyone could have been driving. I knew she had made that up because it isn't illegal to have tinted windows at a certain level. It was how the car was made. I was irritated by her approach. The police car initially in front of us could clearly see we were Black, and they were using the tints as an excuse. I could see how situations escalate. I tried to stay calm and explain to her how profiling was wrong. I told her that something was very wrong if you can't drive around and enjoy a sunny Sunday afternoon if you're Black because the police will view you as suspicious. Section 163 of the Road Traffic Act 1998 allows people to be pulled over by police on the roads, yet they don't have to record the ethnicity of the drivers who are stopped. It is used around 5.5 million times a year, and has masked inequality and discrimination in the system for too long. It needs to change.

I didn't know then what I was going to do with my footage or the information as I really was just recording for research. But the female and the young male police officer were so problematic that I thought I had no choice but to go public, to use my platform to outline what was wrong with the system. This to me was, and always has been, about human rights and dignity.

I posted the video, planning to deal with it the next day, but it immediately went viral online, and the conspiracy theories were off the scale. I still receive abuse about it today. Some said I reversed the footage so it looked as if I was the driver; I didn't even know what they meant until my office pointed out that I was recording in selfie mode, which had made the video appear reversed. The craziest conspiracy of all was that the driver was white, not Black. This theory was propagated by ex-police officers and an apparent detective on Twitter: *If that guy really was a detective*, I thought, *all his cases should be urgently reviewed*. And then someone started a petition for me or the police to release the full video. My friend in the vehicle did not want to be identified – who would, when you see the abuse online? But I was perfectly happy for the police to release their body-worn camera video (BWV) and I wrote to the police saying exactly that – on numerous occasions. There was nothing for me to hide.

My rare day off was ruined. Why couldn't people just believe me, or the evidence put before them?

My inbox was full, and the people who wrote to me mainly fell into three categories: (1) those who knew what it was like to be stopped and searched and were shocked that it could happen to an MP; (2) those who were shocked that this happened every day to Black people; and (3) those who were abusive on Twitter or email, who defended the police at all costs, and/or those who disliked me and my politics.

The prime minister at the time, Boris Johnson, had this to say:

> The police have made a statement saying that they made a mistake. They've spoken to the occupants of the car but it's obviously very, very important that the Met continue to do everything that they can – as indeed they do – to show that they are serving every part of our country, every part of our community, with fairness and equality.[4]

After the stop, I spoke to the commissioner, Cressida Dick, who was still in complete denial about institutional racism, although the police apologized for the mistake they had made. I accepted that apology until a further statement was posted on 12 August 2020:

Deputy Commissioner Sir Steve House has delivered a statement in support of the officers who stopped a vehicle in Hackney last Sunday and also condemns the online abuse that Dawn Butler MP has received.

The stop of a car in which Dawn Butler MP was travelling by Met officers on Sunday has prompted a lot of debate and it is important that the facts are fully understood.

I have viewed all the available video material of that interaction and I have read their statements – the officers acted professionally and politely, explaining why the stop was made and, when realizing there was a mistake, explaining this and continuing to answer the occupants' questions.

I am grateful to these officers, as I am to all our officers who act professionally, humanely and in the service of the public.

I would also like to condemn the abuse that some on social media have directed at Ms Butler. It is unwarranted and unacceptable and we are working to support her.[5]

This statement acted as a dog whistle to extreme right-wing racists, and the abuse towards me increased. I started receiving death threats. In the rush to defend his officers, the deputy commissioner had put my life in danger. I wrote to him two days later as I wanted him to understand the consequences of his actions. The police, of all institutions, should understand consequences.

Dear Sir Stephen,

I am writing to you regarding the recent statement you released on August 12th regarding the Metropolitan Police's decision to stop the car I was in, driving through Hackney last Sunday.

I must say first and foremost that your statement came as something of a surprise as we had only spoken the day before regarding the incident. It was clear from our telephone conversation that, as per your own admission, your officers had incorrectly entered the vehicle registration returning a Silver Toyota Yaris registered in North Yorkshire, the only similarity to our vehicle being its colour. This had been verified by your own queries on the National Police Computer's transaction log. Furthermore, you acknowledged that officers had not properly scrutinized the output from the National Police Computer, a Toyota Yaris evidently being entirely and easily differentiable from a BMW, and thus incorrectly making the decision to pull aside our vehicle.

Given that we had already spoken, and admission made of mistakes on the part of your officers, your statement felt wholly unnecessary to me especially given that the Metropolitan Police had already made an official statement prior. I had also made it clear that I had no problem with the stop, I was querying the reason for the stop. Unfortunately, in the days following your statement I have experienced a serious increase in abuse. Whilst I am sure this was not your intent it is nonetheless the consequence of your statement. You claim to have been writing to clarify some of the issues, but one of the main issues which led to so much of my abuse is the conspiracy theory that the driver is white, and I am surprised that you did not clarify this important fact in your statement.

Can you also confirm, or otherwise, whether it is standard practice for officers to remove the keys from the driver of a vehicle during a traffic stop?

It would have been appreciated, and appropriate, for you to give forewarning of your statement.

As you will know, I recently had a meeting with the Commissioner and we both agreed that due to this unfortunate increase in abuse the Met Police will make a formal statement to corroborate that the driver of the vehicle is a Black male. Due to the vociferous nature of the conspiracy theories circulating as to the vehicle stop, it would be appreciated if you could issue an urgent instruction for this corroborating statement to be released ASAP.

This, I hope, will help to dispel some of the misinformation circulating regarding this situation.

It is with regret however that I was placed in a position at all whereby I had to make this request of the Commissioner. Your statement, I believe, was a missed opportunity to set the record straight and this was an important omission on your part. I would also add that your statement does not appear to give a full account of the incident that occurred. You mention in particular the presence of one vehicle, suggesting officers were unable to see into my friend's car. You have completely disregarded the presence of the second marked police vehicle directly in front of us that then performed a U-turn ending up behind the unmarked police car during the stop. It is for this reason that I explicitly requested release of dash cam footage from the police vehicles.

I understand from our conversation that you were fairly certain neither police vehicles had dash cam installed. However, I am requesting that you follow up on this point and come back to me with absolute clarification on whether there is, or is not, dash cam footage available in both police vehicles. If the footage does exist, I am requesting that you make this available to me. I hope that going forward we can work together to do the very important and necessary work to look at stop and search, and indeed the broad range of powers available to the Met Police, to ensure they are used in a way that is not inherently discriminatory or which has a marginalizing effect on Black, Asian and Minority Ethnic Communities.

I am aware that there have been calls from some quarters to release the Body Worn Camera footage, which I have since reviewed with the Chief Superintendent. To clarify, as long as my friend's face, voice and identity are not revealed I have no objection to its release in the public domain if this is so wished by you, your officers, or their union reps.

Finally, I reserve my right to make this letter public at any point.

Yours sincerely,
Dawn Butler

*

Once I was able to view the body-worn camera footage, it confirmed that at least two police vehicles had been involved in the stop, which the police had at first denied. I actually breathed a sigh of relief. This was important because at least people would begin to believe that the police in the car in front saw the occupants in the vehicle behind them, and therefore knew we were indeed Black. This now became a fuller enquiry for me as to why the police had initially denied it and why it was so important for them to defend themselves rather than fix the problem.

The deputy commissioner wrote back to me on 25 August 2020, confirming that the Metropolitan Police vehicle directly involved in the stop was not fitted with a dash cam, and neither was the second marked police vehicle. He also confirmed that he would not be releasing the footage as it did not provide insight into the motivation for the stop. It seemed strange to me that police cars that are involved day in and day out in vehicle stops were not fitted with dash cams. Surely that should be standard. It's an important part of the job and provides vital evidence. Throughout this whole episode, my primary focus was to ensure a fair system that protects the individual liberty of everyone and is free from bias and discrimination.

A few more letters were exchanged between me and Sir Stephen over the next month as his every response showed that more facts needed clarification. I also wanted to highlight to him that his statement had sparked a petition seeking to remove me as an MP. The pressure I was under was colossal and, after the correspondence back and forth, I was tired and wanted to give up. Why did I have to fight so hard to get to the truth? The fact of the matter was that my friend and I were stopped and surrounded by an unmarked and a marked police car with flashing blue lights – passers-by must have thought the police had some big bust on their hands! We witnessed people slowing down and staring at us. A third car was involved in our stop, but I didn't have that recorded and no one would admit to it. The only thing that kept me going was the knowledge that I was telling the truth and that the system needed to change.

Why is it that the person telling the truth is subjected to more scrutiny than the system or the institution? What is it that makes some people reluctant to criticize the system or admit that those within it can be wrong? Is it because they have never seen a flying cockroach? Or is it because the system has always worked as it was designed to do, benefiting or protecting certain people, criminalizing or disenfranchising others?

It was painfully slow to get the truth out of the police. To force some sort of system change, I made an official complaint. I received a comprehensive fourteen-page reply. (See the Appendix, page 217, for my response.) In addition to this, I was invited to attend a police training programme, which was decent but inadequate when it came to teaching about biases. I sent the training academy copies of *Biased* by Jennifer Eberhardt: she had spent several decades studying policing and biases. Her book is a must-read for anyone wanting to learn more, a police officer or not. When you are trying to change an institution that is old and clunky, in which its members often close ranks to protect their own, it takes much patience. You are often trying to change something that many people are very protective of so it isn't as simple as telling the truth or showing them where they're wrong. As well, you need those at the top to be willing to change: without that, change will never happen to any great extent.

*

Ingrained beliefs, decades in the making, can't be undone easily. When you're challenging an institution, one of the many problems you will face is its support network, which is often well established, well connected and powerful. Soon after I posted the video of my stop, I was invited to do an interview with husband-and-wife Eamonn Holmes and Ruth Langsford of *This Morning* via Zoom. I have had interviews with Eamonn before and we have always been cool. Before going live, I was accidentally joined into the call (I'm not sure by whom) and witnessed private comments and actions that revealed the hosts' exasperation at my incident. I sent a message to my team telling them I could hear and see what Eamonn and Ruth were saying about me. I was cut off from the call once someone realized that I was present, and I knew then that the interview was going to be somewhat hostile.

You can view the interview on YouTube, but at one

point I ask Eamonn to imagine being stopped frequently by the police because of his skin colour. He responds that, as a young Catholic man in Northern Ireland, he was stopped by the police between the ages of seventeen and twenty-six whenever he visited Nationalist areas. He then tells me that there are two ways to deal with being stopped and searched – 'That one either accepts it, realizing that they've done nothing wrong, and you accept what may be termed as "harassment",' he said, with his fingers in air-quotes, 'or you realize that's where a lot of the trouble was emanating from or happening in those areas and that's why you were being stopped or you reacted against it and basically got yourself a charge or arrested.' He then proceeds to tell me that he 'witnessed it all' and that what I experienced that day was nothing in comparison.[6]

To have picked apart and debated his argument would have served no purpose. I was already forewarned that it was going to be a hostile interview so I stayed silent on his point: three minutes is not enough time to explain his misrepresentation. But the fact is that stop-and-search traumatized a lot of communities in Northern Ireland, and we are still dealing with the legacy of the Troubles, including many investigations. The Catholic community did not just sit there and allow stop-and-search: they fought back, including riots after search operations. To this day, there is still mistrust between the Catholic community and the Police Service of Northern Ireland (PSNI) due to the Troubles.

Critically, Eamonn was also referring to *everyone* being searched in a particular area – it wasn't subjective. If everyone was stopped as they entered Hackney, it would have been a completely different situation. We would not have felt so singled out.

If Eamonn and Ruth had taken time to consider where I was coming from they might have come to a different position, but instead I was viewed as the troublemaker and the knee-jerk response was to defend the institution.

I felt I was being talked down to and lectured on the proper way to handle discrimination. The intent of the interview was never about listening and attempting to understand the lived experience of Black people. Rather, it seemed to be about putting me in my place. Eamonn went on to say that I'd 'created such a stir and that everybody is talking about this now'. Then he interrogated me about 'what you have achieved', as though I had misbehaved and needed telling off. Ruth didn't say too much, but as I had previously seen her roll her eyes at me, I wasn't expecting much interaction. It takes a lot of resolve to control my frustration and anger, and to avoid showing such reactions in the face of attack. Even if they are valid, I have to ensure I'm not rising to the stereotype of the 'angry black woman'. But when frustration is shown by a white woman, it's often described as passionate or refreshingly authentic.

People ask me time and again how I remain calm in the face of antagonism and hostility during these interviews. First I take a deep breath, then centre myself in my truth and the argument I am putting across. This is essential if I am to make a difference, and I always hope that someone somewhere will hear what I have to say. If I were to rise to that anger, the message would be lost. I'd be ignored and invisible, and the system would remain the same. That's why it's important to rise many levels above to beat down arguments that are meant to discredit me or the experiences of people like me.

What took place in August 2020 goes beyond me. In fact, it was never about me, but about exposing how people of ethnic backgrounds, particularly Black men, are stopped and searched, targeted by police because of unconscious or conscious bias. This is not new, but it is frustrating that we are still having to insist that institutional racism exists. The Macpherson Report of 1999 acknowledged institutional racism after the investigation into the death of Stephen Lawrence, and in 2020, Sadiq Khan launched an action plan to continue tackling the issue within the force. By collaborating with various stakeholders, including the Mayor's Office of Policing and Crime, the Greater London Authority and London's Violence Reduction Unit, along with the Metropolitan Police Service, sessions were conducted with Black Londoners and Black community organizations to listen to and learn from lived experiences.

The record of my stop was central to the Mayor of London's report and supported the initiative for a six-month pilot programme that required officers to record the ethnicity of the people they were stopping in cars. This was a big step forward: approximately 5.5 million traffic stops occur each year, as reported in 2011.[7] (The trial was reported to have ended but when I questioned the new police commissioner, Sir Mark Rowley, he assured me that it will be extended and he has committed himself to ensuring that it becomes part of everyday policing.) This is an important step forward in tackling the systemic discrimination that exists. The recording of stops adds what is referred to as 'friction'. This is a proactive measure that makes officers think about what they are doing. It has been so effective that most of those who recorded their stops did not pull up Black people at a disproportionate rate. So, basically it works!

Although I found it frustrating, I know that the interview I did on *This Morning* changed some viewers' minds: people emailed my office to say that they hadn't known such things were happening so frequently. At the end of the day, this is not about me but about establishing greater trust between Black people, the system and the police. It's about admitting to a problem and dismantling the biases and behaviours that are still so ingrained in the systems we operate under even today.

So, when Eamonn next asks me what I've achieved, I think it's fair to say, 'Quite a bit. Not only did I raise awareness of what is happening on the streets, I have also managed to change a little bit of the system.'

There are those who don't want to believe institutional racism exists because they think it's out of the realm of possibility in our modern society. But this is a legacy we have inherited from the past. Many people don't see or experience racism in their daily lives. They have never seen a cockroach fly so how can it be possible? But we need to carry on the conversation, dismiss the fantasy that so much has changed, and instead start changing those mindsets: we do not live in a post-racial era. There is still a major problem, yet people tend to discredit the facts, including video evidence, preferring to draw on their own assumptions.

So much of the time, the experiences of Black people are doubted. When something appalling happens, we're asked to prove without a shadow of a doubt that it happened for the reasons we say it did. The onus is on us to bend over backwards to explain what took place and what continually takes place, either to us or to people like us. Yet still, the reaction from some is doubt. Again, it reminds me of what happened with George Floyd. If someone were explaining the incident without the video footage, a certain group of people would feel a strong need to find a reason for the murder – that a man was killed inhumanely because of racism and bigotry will never be enough. They will say, 'Are you sure? Wasn't he under the influence of something?' or 'But wasn't he aggressive?' or 'I don't think that really happened ...' But because Floyd's death was tragically caught on video, it became difficult to 'justify' his killing.

I often wonder why people still refuse to believe in discrimination. Why do they hide from the truth, needing justifiable reasons and evidence? Often there are none, just the lived traumatic experience of the person telling the story. I wonder whether it's because they don't want to, or feel they can't, do anything about it. But since not everyone can go and fetch their dad to tell the adult the truth, or exchange letters with the deputy commissioner of the Metropolitan Police to get an admission of the truth, it falls on all of us to ask ourselves: what are you going to do to help progress the conversation? How are you going to help make society a better place for everyone? Because that's the barrier we need to get across as a nation and it's hard: people are more comfortable believing there's always something more to the story. They're much more content to believe it has nothing to do with them and that the system is working as it should. They'd rather leave it at that than help to create change because it doesn't really affect them or the ones they love. But as we are one human race, what affects one affects us all, sooner or later.

Discrimination in all its forms is destructive, and in some cases it can kill. A woman is killed every three days by a man. Shockingly, Sarah Everard was murdered by a serving police officer, and a prolific rapist was also revealed to be a serving police officer in the Met. These are officers who were trusted. How did they get away with it for so long? These actions do not happen in a vacuum. They happen because society is inherently misogynistic. We will start to make society safer for women if we expose misogynistic language and behaviour. In addition to teaching women and girls how to be safe, we must teach boys and men how to respect and protect women and each other, and how to expose the unacceptable behaviour of other men. If we are to build a society that accepts – not tolerates – people for who they are, then every one of us must work to make it happen.

We need to ask ourselves what our values are and determine what our purpose should be, no matter who we are. You could be a lollipop person walking children across the road or a parent at a coffee morning. If you witness racism, misogyny, homophobia, transphobia, it needs to be called out. Once you are used to accepting people for who they are, it really does make society better, trust me.

*

The Metropolitan Police has been in special measures since June 2022, meaning it is basically on probation as an institution. It's now required that the force put together a plan to address its shortcomings. It is exhausting trying to explain how structurally unsound the system is, but with each high-profile case a different group of people begins to wake up.

In Barking and Dagenham, the police refused to believe the word of the gay community and failed to carry out basic checks or to examine evidence properly in the run-up to the 2016 conviction of serial killer Stephen Port. Four people died because of the homophobic attitude of the police, and in 2022 the Met was reinvestigated over its negligence. I've already mentioned Sarah Everard, who was brutally kidnapped, raped and murdered in 2021 by serving police officer Wayne Couzens. Chris Kaba was fatally shot in the head by police in 2022; he was unarmed and not named as a suspect prior to the incident.

The brutal murder of sisters Bibaa Henry and Nicole Smallman in Brent also shone a light on Metropolitan Police failings, with police taking too long to act, leaving family members and friends to find the sisters' bodies after they had gone missing. The institutional racism and misogyny that exists in the force were laid bare when two police officers took photos of their bodies and shared the images on WhatsApp groups, for which they have since been jailed. I was heartbroken that the family had to go through that trauma at the hands of those they were supposed to trust, having already lost their beautiful daughters. Their mother, Mina, told me that the police betrayal hurt.

Then there was the dehumanizing strip-search of Child Q and the stop, search and use of handcuffs with Team GB sprinter Bianca Williams and her partner Ricardo dos Santos, all while their young baby was in a seat at the back of the car. Ricardo ended up buying a Tesla so that he could record any subsequent stops. What he didn't realize was that at his next stop he would be surrounded by several armed officers.

So many more such stories have been uncovered, all grave examples of a serious problem. For those whose first reaction is to protect the institution no matter what, loyalties will now need to be examined. The police sticking together to protect each other does not protect the general public. We need a system in which misconduct is exposed not just by the public but by police officers. Too often this has not been the case. I think this is what many good, honest officers want too. Now, in 2023, the Casey Report has found the Metropolitan Police to be institutionally racist, misogynist and homophobic. Yet still, at the time of writing, the new commissioner has refused to accept the term 'institutionally racist'.

As a society, if we can't look critically at a system and say it's not working as well as it should, if we can't acknowledge that change is needed, or call out bad behaviour, especially when it pertains to an often-impenetrable boys' club, if we can't criticize constructively, who are these systems really for? It's time to grow up and take responsibility, to address difficult issues and tackle them head-on, even if it feels scary.

I remember once being the only Black person around the table at a meeting. We were talking about giving the police extra powers, and my colleagues were getting really excited about the policies they wanted to put into place. They believed that allowing the police to do whatever they wanted, without question or accountability, would help stop crime.

I kept quiet for as long as I could, trying gently to interject and then, although it felt scary, I said something like 'What you all think is a brilliant idea and are getting very excited about is actually scaring me.' Those people did not know Black men the way I did, and for me, the conversation immediately brought to mind my four brothers and how their lives would be negatively impacted by these new measures. But the home secretary at the time and other ministers were all looking through a different lens. My presence in that room provided a very different insight. Although it was hard for me to speak up that day, I was listened to, and the police didn't get the powers they wanted. (The current government tried to implement some of the same measures during Covid. As a result, Black people were stopped 22,000[8] times during the pandemic and were statistically twice as likely to be fined as their white counterparts.)

When trying to implement real and lasting change, not only do we have to set aside our fear and speak up about injustice, no matter how large the institution or how overwhelming the pushback may be, we also need to understand exactly how the system works, and why things are done as they are. Thanks to my diligence in recording and questioning my traffic stop, I managed to bring about change, with the Metropolitan Police running a trial to record all traffic stops.

Because this change is disrupting the status quo, you'll also properly understand the consequences if it isn't followed correctly, and see how an easy override could exacerbate the problem. In my particular stop, when I asked for the footage from the younger police officer, I was informed that he didn't have on his body-worn camera because of what I would later learn was a dead battery. If it has been agreed that one of the ways to protect potential victims from police brutality and injustice is for officers to wear a camera, it's an easy yet dangerous over-ride that they can go around with uncharged ones. There should be an institution-wide policy to ensure that they are on and fully charged before every shift. Otherwise there is nothing to prevent them from being deliberately misused.

This is tiring work, but we have to be relentless in our conversations around injustice, whether it is police reform or abuse in the workplace, school or home. It's only by knowing our truth, knowing how the systems work, and being persistent in our questioning that we can hold perpetrators to account.

4

NOT YOUR NORMAL
POLITICIAN

People often tell me I'm not your normal politician – I didn't go to university or study PPE or work as a special adviser before becoming an MP. Instead, I've had real-life experiences, all of which have made me who I am today.

Thanks to my computer teacher, Mr Taylor, who encouraged me to buckle down, I was inspired to study computing at Waltham Forest College after I left school. I met one of my best friends, Claudia, at the entrance exams. She looked as if she needed a friend, so as I finished early I lingered by the door, introducing myself as if I'd been to the college before and knew my way around. It felt right to let her know that someone was on her side, another young woman in a course full of mainly young men, another person roughly of her background.

There was a group of us, a crew of young people across Greek, African, Turkish, Asian and Jamaican heritage. We grew close, spending late afternoons at the local YMCA, playing board games or grabbing some food at

Pizza Hut during our lunch breaks. On one occasion, returning to college just a minute or two late, we found ourselves locked out of the classroom by a stern lecturer. Her reaction felt extreme to me, and I reasoned with her on behalf of the group, telling her the bus had been late. Eventually, she let us in.

It wasn't unusual for me to find myself assuming a leadership role – I guess it came naturally to me – but leadership was nothing without teamwork and collaboration, without listening to the opinions of my peers. I never wanted to assert my own beliefs over those of the others.

College was where I first took an interest in British Sign Language (BSL). We had two deaf students on our course, and although we spent most of our time in front of computers coding, I wanted to include them in my madness, and in the conversations the rest of us were having. I taught myself rudimentary chat, but when I became a civil servant some years later, and worked alongside a deaf colleague, I took evening classes, achieving a BSL level-two qualification. (Level three was for those who wanted to be interpreters.)

My journey would come full circle as an MP when in March 2017, the day before the fourteenth anniversary of the official recognition of BSL, I became the first MP to ask a question in sign language in the House of Commons. I had rehearsed with my local Brent and Harrow United Deaf Club and fellow MP, Rosie Cooper. (She is a child of deaf parents, and profoundly deaf herself, but her hearing aids allow her to hear and be heard.) When I took my seat on that historic day, another Labour colleague, Rachel Maskell, signed to me when I sat next to her, which was a great surprise. I wanted to raise awareness of BSL and ask the minister to bring forward a Bill that would give BSL full legal status in Britain. Rosie eventually introduced the British Sign Language Act 2022. It requires the secretary of state for work and pensions to produce regular reports on what twenty government departments have done to 'promote or facilitate' the use of BSL, and for guidance to be issued in relation to BSL.

I wouldn't have had an interest in BSL if I hadn't been exposed to it in college. It was one of the first times I became aware of my own privilege and could see how the world was designed for the hearing. Once again, I was reminded of the importance of allies and advocating for others. If you can open your mind to difference, the role you can play in society through using your privilege can create a wave of change.

*

After college, Claudia and I thought we'd apply for a few top jobs we saw in the papers. We never expected to get any, and decided that, once our applications were rejected, we'd move on and apply for university instead. Surprisingly, Claudia went to work at a bank, and I ended up as a computer programmer for a City firm. My experience working in the City was the first time I'd come face to face with what it meant to be a lone woman in a male-dominated environment. I'd also learn that although coding was a perfect fit for my brain, it wasn't quite the perfect fit for my activism.

My first proper office job was an adjustment on quite a few levels. I have never been a stranger to the company of men – after all I spent loads of time with my brothers and was used to the friendship of young men at the college. But being the only woman on a small team of four, where I was suddenly being sexualized, was different. It was a rude awakening.

One guy in particular made me feel very uncomfortable. He never let up on the sexual innuendos or the inappropriate actions, like dropping pencils on the floor as an excuse to look up my skirt. His behaviour was seen as 'banter' by my co-workers, and I was expected to suck it up, which I did. When I finally complained to HR, it was made clear to me that they would do nothing about my colleague's actions, so I wore trousers to get through my days.

This is often the problem with sexual harassment. It's always the victim who's required to adjust their behaviour to mitigate the situation, rather than the person perpetrating the abuse. The trousers were a temporary fix: he made my life a living hell for many years.

I stopped feeling good every time I came to work. I was unhappy, and the harassment was affecting my work as a programmer. I lost interest in what I'd been hired to do because I was so focused on keeping myself safe. There was another guy on the team who I was closer to than I was to the rest, but he never intervened, and they would say things of my tormentor like 'He's just a bit of an idiot,' without taking on board how his behaviour made me feel.

I wanted my co-workers to have my back in the way my brothers did. In those moments I needed someone bold enough to stamp out their colleague's bad behaviour. And I needed a system that protected women, but I was young, and in those days, it was difficult for men to call their friends out for fear of being bullied or seen as 'weak'. You still see this happening today, not just on a personal level, but within our larger institutions, which continually fail to punish men for bad behaviour, let alone call them out early on.

Sometimes if bad behaviour is called out, people are accused of being 'woke'. This is one reason why I'm such an activist today and have no shame around using such a word. It's important that society speaks out against abusive people and, in particular, abusive men. Someone like Wayne Couzens, the ex-police officer who killed Sarah Everard, didn't start with murder, he started with racist and misogynistic WhatsApp messages, then exposed himself in public. The police system protected him until it was too late to stop him.

When the company I worked for began restructuring after five years, I jumped at the chance to leave and took redundancy. I didn't look for another job, and I wasn't in a hurry to find one. I took a whole year out. I look back now and realize I was healing myself – as a young person, I thought I was resilient, but I discovered I had been routinely worn down for years. The powerlessness I felt during that time had destabilized me, a strange thing to accept because I thought I was quite formidable. Working with my colleagues in a system that couldn't support me had shaken me. I had done everything I possibly could during a time when sexual harassment wasn't taken seriously – I complained to management, wore trousers and tried to appeal to the perpetrator's better nature – but I couldn't resolve the issue.

For the first time in my life I discovered it's not always possible to conquer some of your individual problems when the system and structure are much bigger than you. Sometimes, when you're fighting the system and you're not winning, you've either got to change yourself to fit within it or come out of it to protect yourself from elements that are particularly harmful.

But years of experience have also shown me that, although you may never be able to conquer what's wrong with the system, you might still be able to achieve, in your initial actions, a slow wearing down of its problems. A bit like when you're trying to open a bottle of ketchup. The first person to try might not succeed, but the fourth accomplishes it because everyone else has loosened the lid a little. When you're fighting injustice, your efforts are never wasted, even if it feels that way, and that's something I tell myself every single day.

So much has changed over the last thirty years, especially when it comes to sexual harassment in the workplace, but back in the day it was a difficult thing for my male colleagues to acknowledge or tackle. When I eventually found my way into Parliament, I would soon learn that women, too, could downplay certain behaviours and discredit valid feelings of discomfort.

Recently a well-known actress said that women are too soft: in her day they used to brush away the wandering hands. That's not very helpful to the progress we're trying to make. A woman should never have to be subject to unwanted touching, or policed around what she chooses to wear. Early on in my political career, I walked into Parliament wearing fishnet tights. I had spent the night at my mum's place, and in the morning, as I got ready for work, I threw on an outfit of hers. (Mum has great taste – we've even got some of the same clothes.) To an old-school Jamaican, it was taboo to leave the house with bare legs, and she *insisted* I wear tights before heading off too. But the only pairs she had were fishnets, which she loves.

I hadn't put too much thought into my decision until I arrived at work, and soon regretted it. It's been well documented that Black women are often fetishized, and as one of two Black female MPs at the time, I had Labour and Conservative MPs making sexualized comments at me. I might have laughed after the first couple of comments (someone asked if my fishnet tights came with a whip), but the unwanted attention grew too intense. It was a bit like wearing trousers to avoid an uncomfortable situation, but this time I had female colleagues to speak to, more senior MPs who, I assumed, would sympathize with me. I was told it was just a joke, and I needed to toughen up if I was going to survive that place. I was told I couldn't take every little thing to heart and was made to feel stupid for wearing the tights, and for sharing my discomfort. After receiving such unhelpful advice from multiple female colleagues, I stopped asking for support. I needed to clear my head and figure out how I was going to deal with it. (It wasn't the last time I was disappointed by lack of support from my peers.)

I spoke to my friend Lynda Waltho, MP, and later confided in Sadiq Khan, who offered, jokingly, to beat someone up, and it was the cheering up I needed. I couldn't take on every battle. I went to the women's loo to throw the tights into the bin. But what a shame that, early in my working life, I was told time and again that a woman needed to present herself in a particular way if she wanted to be taken seriously, not to mention the different standards that apply to Black women. (Kelechi Okafor's comedy series on Instagram called 'Sally in HR' makes the point with humour when Sally calls in a Black woman and informs her that the black dress she's wearing is inappropriate for work because it's too sexy. Sally mutters under her breath that she has the same dress, and it doesn't look *that* way on her.) In any case, since the fishnet-tights episode, I have changed my mind about needing to conform, deciding to wear whatever I feel like, and opting these days for the brightest and boldest outfits imaginable.

*

I spent much of my year of healing raising money for charities – I am an awesome organizer and used to put on talent shows with my friend Alan. We once raised money to send a young boy with cerebral palsy to the Pedro Institute in Germany for treatment. We auditioned singers, hired a live band, and hosted the evenings at Walthamstow town hall where we brought in a packed audience to vote for the winner. Afterwards, we'd arrange for that lucky person to have a free recording session. Raising money for charity was fun and felt good, but Mum, in so many words, pointed out that I needed to earn some money or I'd never leave home. I didn't want to go back to programming, so I started looking for something more aligned with my values.

The first thing I thought to do was go to the Job Centre to get help with a new CV. When you request this service, you also have to sign on, and I soon received a letter telling me to go for an interview. Because I was used to working in the City, the word 'interview' meant I got suited and booted. I brought along a nice little leather briefcase, which had taken me months to save up for, and when I walked into the Job Centre offices, they thought I had come to interview for a job in the employment service, not an interview to sign on. Their mistake meant I was ushered into a different office and made to take a test. In the end, I was hired as a manager. The entire experience was quite surreal, but it spoke to the idea of dressing for the job you want.

As a manager, the first thing I did was to encourage my entire team to join a trade union. I could see the cogs turning in their heads, wondering why on earth I'd tell them to do that, and whether this meant I'd be the worst boss ever. It took them a while to understand I was doing this for their own safety, protection and peace of mind. No matter how much strength I thought I had in my own situation or how much fight, I'd found that when a hell of a lot was coming at me, it was impossible for me to tackle it on my own. Black women are often taught to be strong, and this strength is also assumed by others, so it's difficult for many of us to ask for or accept help, whether from a friend, a therapist, or an organization. Trade unions help individuals amplify their voice for systemic change.

I led on a membership drive in the Job Centre and watched as numbers grew. Managers weren't supposed to do things like that, but I felt it was right, especially after my own experience in the corporate world. An opportunity arose for me to go to a trade-union conference when a colleague who broke their leg could no longer attend. The experience was intense but a lot of fun, and completely opened my eyes. The powerhouse that was Mary Turner, an inspiration to many in the movement, who became president of the GMB (Britain's

General Union) in 1997, taught me how to drink vodka responsibly, and drink everyone else under the table. We worked hard but we played hard too, and it spurred me to become more active, perhaps too much so: some felt I was coming in to upset the status quo.

What struck me most was that people of colour made up most of the membership, but the leadership was principally white and male. That didn't make sense to me. I often viewed my dad as an unofficial trade-union representative as people went to him for guidance at work, but he was never encouraged or supported to stand for an official position.

Once I became a full-time official and saw another side to the movement, I understood that perfect organizations rarely exist, even if they are created to tackle inequalities. Understanding that a lot needed to be done to correct this, I joined the Black caucus within the union, and when a position for chair became available, I went for it. I thought I could do things differently, as I always tend to do. In the end, they gave the chair to someone else, but created a position for me along the lines of deputy chair. I think it was a case of 'She might be useful but let's test her out first.'

Over the course of many years, I worked for several unions and was the first recruitment officer for the Public and Commercial Services Union (PCS). I was then head-hunted and became the national race officer for the GMB, where I met the general secretary, Paul Kenny, for the first time. I bounced into his office with a rucksack on my back and sat down, and I remember Paul smiling. He later said people were normally a bit scared to meet him, but he knew from the off that I was going to be good. Looking back, Paul reminded me of Mr Taylor – he just got me. He knew what I could achieve and would leave me to it. To this day I still ring Paul for advice.

As a full-time officer, I organized for us to have a race audit – the first any union had ever commissioned. I put forward recommendations to be implemented, such as the development of a national recruitment strategy involving targets for BAME membership that reflected the makeup of local communities, and a positive action programme meant to provide opportunities for BAME groups to join in at all levels of the union, including activist, membership and employee levels, whether that be training, shadowing or meeting with community groups to determine the barriers to involvement. Many of the recommendations I put forward are still valid today.

The trade unions have changed a lot since I first joined, but as with many of our institutions, there is always more that could be done. We must never stop learning and evolving because that is how we progress. It was interesting moving from the outside as a union activist to the inside as a union official: my view of the organization was different depending on where I stood. (I would later have a similar experience in Parliament.) While working for the GMB, I received a piece of advice that has served me well throughout my life. When I was uncompromising, wanting to take the whole system down, I was told (probably by Paul, actually) to pick my battles. Looking back, I would have added, 'Be kind to yourself, Dawn, and give yourself more time. Just because you can doesn't always mean you should. Let someone else sometimes pick up the slack.'

*

My friend Dawn Faniku once observed that every five years I tend to make a life-changing decision, and in 2003, I did this when I was asked by a trade unionist to stand as a Labour parliamentary candidate for Hackney South and Shoreditch. The people who approached me envisaged a socialist and trade unionist as the candidate. My initial response to this was no! *Why would I want to be a politician?* Politicians, from what I could see, were either white and/or male: there were only two Black female MPs at that time – Diane Abbott and Oona King. That's two out of 650.

It wasn't just a colour thing, it was a class thing, too. Not only was I working class, but I was also a trade unionist. I wasn't posh, and I hadn't gone to university. Parliament wasn't an institution for people like me. I didn't think politicians were bad people, I just thought the job wouldn't be my cup of tea, but my supporters wouldn't take no for an answer. 'There are no guarantees of winning,' they said, but recommended I should throw my hat into the ring.

As usual, I turned to my family for advice. The responses were mixed. Mum, who usually said no to everything and was always the cautious parent, muttered something like 'What's she up to now?' My dad, who always had dreams beyond measure for me, was all for it, although he would have preferred me to be a television or news presenter. Sadly for him, that particular dream was dashed when my friend Alan and I went for an audition to be children's presenters and didn't get the job.

I have always loved the energy of children, and thought being a presenter would be the perfect job, but in those days, I think it was too early for broadcasters to visualize *too* many Black presenters on TV. Floella Benjamin, now a Lib Dem peer in the House of Lords, was already breaking new ground. When I met her later in life, my love of her children's show ensured that we had a mutual respect, and when she was expected by her party to attack me during the 2010 campaign, she refused. That is what solidarity looks like. And I will always respect her for the stance she took.

Back to 2003, and I gathered a few more opinions, thought about my prospects in the trade unions, and eventually decided to go for the candidacy, but it wasn't a decision I took lightly. Paul had told me that the GMB were not very organized as a union with regard to helping trade unionists become candidates. There were no formal processes in place until I went for it, so Hackney South and Shoreditch was a crash course on what it took to stand and what was needed to campaign. I entered the race late, and by that point most of the Labour members were supporting other candidates, like Dora Dixon-Fyle and

Meg Hillier, to name just two. We were on an all-women shortlist, an affirmative action strategy introduced by the Labour Party in the 1990s to increase the number of women MPs. They'd found that even when women entered the selection process, the men were routinely chosen, whether they were good or not. I often say that we'll know when we've reached true equality when we have as many useless women as we do useless men in Parliament.

I gathered my team and found that people who simply liked what I was about joined my campaign, and that was the most humbling and surprising aspect for me. I felt like I had the wind at my back because people believed in my vision and rallied around me. That gave me strength when the responsibilities of campaigning felt relentless – every day I knocked on doors, convincing Labour Party members within the borough to vote for me. They were thorough in their questioning, leaving no stone unturned. They wanted to know why I would be the best candidate, and each time I met someone new, I hoped I had left a bit of me with them. I enjoyed this part of the campaign because I liked talking to people, and could connect with them on different levels, through music, dance, politics and what-have-you.

My first campaign never came with any expectations. I wanted to win, of course I did, but jumping in so late made it almost impossible. I had watched Dora Dixon-Fyle's race closely, and at one point I thought she could have come first, but it would be Meg Hillier, who had been a member of the London Assembly and lived locally, who would eventually win. She is still the MP for Hackney South and Shoreditch.

Politics is a numbers game. It's also about timing, luck and skill. Importantly, being mindful of party structures is also a must, and this was something I would come to learn the hard way. In 2005, not long after Hackney South and Shoreditch, I put myself forward for West Ham when Labour MP Tony Banks retired. This time I felt ready as I had done it once before. I applied what I had learned from my first campaign and started organizing early. Paul said I could work flexibly so I was given the green light, although he still didn't think I would win because, through his investigations, he had learned that the position was earmarked for someone else. He made it clear that he wasn't going to stop me, though – I think he was fascinated by my drive and determination and wanted to see me win, particularly as it had been the seat of Will Thorne, founder of the GMB, many moons ago.

The people who supported me on my previous campaign came with me to West Ham. They helped me deliver leaflets and knock on doors. They could speak to people on my behalf because by then they knew a bit about what drove me. And that is a useful lesson. If you can connect with people in a meaningful and positive way, they will be with you on your life's journey. Unfortunately, I lost the selection by four votes. I felt this defeat differently from the first. Then, I hadn't minded losing because I had never expected to win. The second time I lost, I felt cheated. It was nothing against Lyn Brown – she and I get on incredibly well and she is a loving, caring person, one of the best in Parliament – but I felt there was something seriously wrong and unfair with our selection system.

Those who are familiar with my politics, who have heard my speeches or who follow me on social media, will have heard me say by now, 'I don't lose, I learn.' It's an active choice to hold on to the positives of what an experience has given you. Those two races (and many others along the way) taught me the importance of stating your intentions early and planning accordingly. This applies to politics, but it can also apply to other situations, like a promotion or transitioning careers, or whatever you're trying to achieve. Speak your goals and ambitions out loud, write them down, and put them somewhere you can see them. Then list the steps you must take to get where you need to be, and find people who will fight your corner. If you can, seek out those who can give you adequate support and advice. (Although I will say, often in politics, people try to cut your legs off before you start, so use discretion when deciding if you should announce your goals early!)

Be inclusive in terms of the people you want to reach out to and gather as much information as you can from as many sources as possible. (Again, a warning here: when it comes to politics, some people can be very duplicitous. For example, when I stood for deputy leader of the Labour Party, an MP came to question me on my future policies and how I would implement them. I spent over an hour speaking to him, so it was a surprise when the candidate he was actually supporting started using my ideas!)

Despite the setbacks I faced from the selection campaigns, the hardships equipped me with the knowledge for the next phase of my journey. Sometimes in life you never know how things will pan out, or why hurdles have been placed in front of you, but it's good practice to keep trying.

*

After losing two races in short succession, I was tired, disappointed and wanted out of politics. I booked tickets to Jamaica and was preparing for a holiday when news broke that the MP Paul Boateng was going to South Africa to be high commissioner. Brent South was now available, and all the people who said I would never make it, who saw how close I had come to winning in West Ham, were now telling me I had to stand. Yet all I wanted was to be left alone. I didn't think I had the energy for another selection, but in the end Paul Kenny said I could use the GMB offices where I worked in Hendon to campaign. Paul believed in me and that gave me the energy I needed to try again. I knew I could do it once I put my mind to it and, with his support and encouragement, I felt it was worth another go.

The seat was earmarked for Tony Blair's special adviser, who was treated as a superstar. He could be seen walking down the road, masses of people surrounding him, cameras everywhere ... and then there was me, with people I had gathered from my previous two campaigns. But I did what I needed to do. I knocked on every single door and talked to every single member and never took anything for granted. I had also worked in Brent, so I had GMB connections, like Mary Turner, behind me. Although campaigning was exhausting, the support of my union was one hell of a boost.

One of the last houses I knocked on was that of Muhammed (Mo) Butt, now leader of Brent Council. It was probably around 8 p.m. when we finally arrived at his house – any time after that and you started to irritate people. (Campaigning is a science: never knock on doors during *EastEnders*, for example.) Mo liked me so much he took me to his brother Saqib's house five doors down, then to his cousin's. My support was gaining traction and my numbers were growing, one member at a time.

By this point in the race, I had become used to the sorts of attacks my opponents launched at me. The fact that I'm unmarried and without kids was a popular one, but I've never felt any shame around my relationship status, and as far as children went, I'd been mothering from the age of eight, when Mum came home from hospital one day and handed me my youngest brother. I've raised a lot of kids in my time and used to miss college to look after my nieces and nephews. I now consider myself a phenomenal aunty, and I own that with all the strength of my being. I have always felt that one of my purposes in life is to be a stable force in my nieces' and nephews' lives, so I was never upset by my opponents' efforts to show me as the weaker candidate because I didn't have kids. Just ask my nephews Sean, Matthew, Curtis and Tyrone, or my nieces Charlene, Maritta and Simone, about the importance of a phenomenal aunty!

But when time came for the hustings, I was nervous and shaking. There were four of us on the shortlist, male and female, and I was following the only other Black female candidate, whom I high-fived as I passed her. Even though we were both after the same seat, we didn't view each other as enemies, just wanted the best for each other. I did my speech, got a great reception, and on my canvassing rounds, I remember people saying to me, 'I don't want to upset Tony Blair, but I will vote for you as long as you don't tell anyone.'

After the ballots were counted, I had won with over 50 per cent of the vote. My data was correct, and I had proven wrong everyone who doubted me or said I couldn't do it. I had taken the learnings from my previous campaigns and focused on each and every member. I had been honest with myself, and I had always ended my day on a high. I was overjoyed, and my knees went weak. The campaign team and camera crew who had put all their energies into Tony Blair's special adviser were stunned and looked like they were going to collapse too. They were relying on politics as usual, forgetting that the power of the people could (on occasion) pull you through. At the end of the day, it's one member one vote (OMOV). I remember thinking, OMG, I beat the system!

I'd never been the chosen one, not for this race and certainly not for the previous two, but I worked hard to show the party I could win without being the preferred candidate. I was a different kind of politician, and I think the people I came across found that refreshing. I knew how to talk to and connect with all kinds of people: the bakery had taught me that. I was also a trade unionist and some people had heard of my work representing dinner ladies. So, at thirty-five years old, I became the third ever Black female MP elected to Parliament, behind Diane Abbott and Oona King, and four years later, in 2009 I made history, becoming the first elected Black female government minister in the House of Commons for Prime Minister Gordon Brown. (Before that, I was the first Black female whip.)

I ensured that young people were able to come into Parliament to debate, despite the pushback from the Tories. I was pleased that the UK Youth Parliament was able to debate in the House of Commons last year, for the first time since 2019, which saw more than two hundred young people aged between eleven and eighteen take part. I remember one MP saying that the House of Commons' green benches were for elected bottoms only – this was technically true, as an actual rule, but it seemed downright petty to me not to allow young people to occupy them.

If we were really going to break down barriers, and let young people see they could be there too, why not let them sit there? In the end, with the support of then-speaker, John Bercow, and others, we were able to get this off the ground.

While I was minister, we invested millions of pounds in youth centres and services, and set about an Agenda for Youth Engagement, recognizing that young people could play an active role as citizens. Even though more and more young people advocate for their future, particularly around climate change, we still fail to prioritize their role in society today. When I talk about community, this includes young people taking part in politics and public services. When it comes to issues directly affecting them, it's important that their voices and ideas are heard, and that they become part of the decision-making processes. The time I spend in schools in my constituency has shown me that some kids care about, and are affected by, many of the same issues that impact adults. This depends on their lived experience and the journeys they have already taken. Apart from children referring to our prime ministers as 'that horrible man/woman' or 'that nice man/woman', they'll speak to me about housing or immigration and how much it costs to make an application for indefinite leave to remain; the issues vary.

It always surprises me how engaged these kids are, but I often find that those who struggle most or who have experienced trauma are the most political. They understand the issues of immigration because they have lived it. Poverty is part of their daily lives, but they don't often connect their activism with traditional politics.

*

My seat in Brent South disappeared in 2010 due to redrawn boundaries. In 2015 it was time to run another campaign and this, too, would be tough. Not many MPs return to Parliament after boundary changes or losing their seat to represent the same area they previously represented. Those of us who do are called retreads. The thing about being an MP is that there is always someone waiting in the wings to replace you. The system didn't forgive me for beating it, and those in charge encouraged as many people as possible to stand against me. Almost a hundred people applied to become a Brent Central candidate.

As the candidate, I was in search of a campaign office, and after moving around a fair bit, a local businessman, Lalgi, offered us a space at 156 High Road, Willesden. The community came together, led by my friends, Guna and Pravin, and helped my team and me redecorate, with another local businessman coming in to put cupboards in the kitchen for us. It was quite cold during those first few months and we had to make do with a portable gas heater. As more and more people joined the campaign, finding enough money to feed my volunteers became difficult. But, once again, local businesses were in action, providing us with free pizza, chicken and chips, and West Indian food – every day someone fed the lot of us and we were grateful.

However, during the selection, my opponents were playing dirty, with one even printing a leaflet insinuating that I didn't do serious politics. I can't quite remember the exact phrasing, but it was something along the lines of 'This isn't a fashion show, this is serious politics.' Throughout my career, I have been given all kinds of advice about the way I dress. People have told me to tone it down and to wear more outfits from Marks & Spencer. I've been told not to be so smiley, and to be softer, because, you know, Black women can be seen as having 'a chip on their shoulder'. I've been told not to be too Black, to leave Black issues at the door because they're seen as too threatening and not inclusive enough (even though I have a track record of being incredibly inclusive in my politics). But my response to all these suggestions – past and present – is simply to be me. At the end of the day, if I were to wake up one morning and not recognize myself, that would really hurt me.

I love my constituency and the people in it. We are a vibrant slice of London and I love being in the heart of the community. I built up a strong following of supporters while I was serving as MP for Brent South, and when my constituents heard I was going to stand again, they were thrilled. As a result, more people joined the party as members to vote for the candidate because, at the end of the day, politics is a numbers game.

A pillar of the Brent community, Dame Betty Asafu-Adjaye, joined the Labour Party around this time to show her unwavering support. She was a beloved figure to many in the area for her work in feeding the sick and elderly, and was known for founding the Mission Dine Club from the kitchen of her flat, until she was awarded a National Lottery grant and was able to rent a place. But someone from the local Labour Party's general committee questioned Dame Betty's reasons for joining the party and queried with her whether she could afford the membership fee – about three pounds per month! Dame Betty was offended and asserted her right to join the Labour Party. A few things felt off to her: were these questions asked of everyone who wanted to join the party? Sometime later, she was told that her application to join had been rejected by the local executive committee. Dame Betty was confused, embarrassed and, not knowing the rules, was ready to give up. She showed the rejection letter to some existing members and was encouraged to ask to see the minutes of the meeting at which her application had been turned down. They apparently proved that her application had been rejected. Still not convinced, Dame Betty and a group of others came to me, and asked if this was something that normally happened. I told them it was unusual and said I would investigate.

It turned out that the local executive meeting had never taken place. The letter had been forged to try to exclude Dame Betty from the party, simply because she was going to vote for me. When I complained to London region about this, the party did nothing about it. It was yet another example of the disappointing side of politics and the system closing ranks. I wouldn't have known about it if Dame Betty hadn't questioned the system with determination. It reiterates why we should not accept seemingly harmless actions that blatantly try to take away our liberties. Sometimes we must find people with the knowledge and power to help us navigate our way through.

Dame Betty became a member. I won Brent Central, and the campaign office we were using in Willesden became my constituency office. Astoundingly, the committee member who initially questioned Dame Betty was still allowed to stand as a councillor and remains a councillor to this day.

It should come as no surprise that at every turn there have been people who never wanted me to succeed. This happens often in politics, but it happens in other systems too. Gatekeepers, people who are more powerful, control the way a system operates. For as long as our systems fail to change, there will always be hurdles for certain kinds of people, but I have learned that they can be jumped over, not just by sheer determination but also by asking for help. I had lots of support; Brent people who I leaned on and helped elevate me like Tullah, James, Lincoln, Saqib, Parvez, Mrs Sewar, Tariq, Kwaku, Dina and so many more. Never be afraid to accept help. It's useful to have someone to go to who is more experienced and knowledgeable about how a system works, a mentor who can help you move past the gatekeepers or at least topple those invisible barriers.

That is exactly what I did when I applied to be a magistrate. I was initially turned down because I had failed to declare the three points I had once had on my driving licence for a long-spent speeding conviction. It had completely slipped my mind, as I had a clean licence. In passing, I spoke to a KC friend, Matthew Ryder, who is the most positive and phenomenal person – he also makes the most amazing ackee and saltfish. I met him early on in my parliamentary career through Sadiq Khan. Matthew wanted to ensure that he connected with people in the Black community so that we all had a network to fall back on, a much-needed space for fellowship and support – the Ryder garden parties are legendary! When I spoke to him about the reason for my rejection as a magistrate, I was embarrassed because I felt as if I'd done something wrong. *I should have known better*, I thought. I blamed myself for not remembering, even though I had no record of the incident now that I had a clean licence.

But Matthew said, 'What are you talking about? Are you crazy? You've got to appeal! You have so much to offer.'

'I'm reluctant,' I said. 'If they don't want me to do it, they don't want me to do it.'

But he pressed the matter and insisted. His experience told him that a twenty-five-year-old spent conviction was no reason to reject my application. And if I appealed I would win. I appealed, and the ruling was overturned. I became a magistrate, but if I hadn't spoken to Matthew, I would have let it go. In him, as in Dame Betty, I had a true advocate, and it goes to show how useful it is to share our injustices with those who will listen, who are in more powerful positions than we are, especially if we think they will care. Not only is there a chance that they will support us but they might challenge us to keep fighting, to keep pushing for what is right. When we don't fit the usual mould, this is how we move the dial on the injustices that exist in society today.

5

NOBODY LIKES THE
R-WORD

My background in computing means I like to ensure systems run as efficiently as possible, which was why I joined the House of Commons Modernization Committee early in my parliamentary career. MPs can join a wide range of committees that look more closely at parliamentary procedures and proposed laws, and examine government departments and other timely topics. It's now discontinued, but with the Modernization Committee, I hoped to contribute ideas that would help Parliament evolve with the times: many of its processes and procedures were (and still are) antiquated.

As you can imagine, there were people on the committee, the Tories especially, who liked the way things were and wanted to ensure that nothing changed. For instance, we were allowed to bring only paper into the chamber and preferably no handbags – very convenient for the men in Parliament. I suspected that many of my colleagues still wanted us to write with quill pens – the old-fashioned way of doing things being a badge of honour! On one occasion, an MP waited at the door to the chamber for the doorkeeper to open it. Why couldn't he open it himself? He didn't even have the manners to say 'Thank you.' Even to this day, some politicians refuse to have an email account and won't respond to constituents unless they make contact via a letter, but we managed to achieve the use of mobile devices in the chamber.

During my time on the committee, I wanted to ensure that incoming MPs had proper training and a mentor. Neither had been in place before. When I joined, you came into Parliament and that was it. I felt there needed to be a lot more care. When you enter Parliament you are officially self-employed, and some MPs had no experience of managing a team, a key part of our role, which caused issues with power dynamics. I have seen a lot go wrong. We are still hearing about sexual harassment in Parliament, or the abuse of power dynamics, for example, and I wanted to help write a new code of conduct as part of the committee. I spent months working tirelessly with MPs from all political parties, and representatives from the GMB and Unite, who represented the staff in the Houses of Commons and Lords to help set up a new independent complaints and grievances scheme, a stronger system to promote better behaviour and improve the culture of our workplace.

Parliament isn't easy, and most MPs are under a lot of pressure. On a day-to-day basis, my team of caseworkers and I received more than two hundred emails from local constituents with issues ranging from immigration to housing. I cannot do my job without my office support. Unlike a lot of MPs, my team, James, Lee, Luc, Shereen and Elijah, have been with me for many years. Having a good team allows me to focus on various things simultaneously. The main areas of work for an MP are Parliament, committees and their constituency. I hold surgeries where constituents can come to talk about anything that matters to them. I'm always very busy: I'm either attending an event, or visiting schools, and if I'm not visiting schools, I'm constantly meeting and speaking to all kinds of people.

Much as I'd experienced when I started my role as a trade-union official, coming into Parliament was very different from what I had imagined. Naively, I assumed everyone would be of the same mindset, that we would all share the same ideas around right and wrong, so it was a rude shock to be faced with overt racism and sexism. I blamed myself during those early years in Parliament – *why hadn't I prepared for such behaviour?* How did I think that an institution hundreds of years old, with only 20 per cent women and 0.3 per cent (just two) Black female MPs in 2005,[1] would protect me against discrimination? I feel silly now when I think about it. On the one hand I wanted to do the job, and understood that my being there could help, in some small way, to make Parliament more representative of the country it seeks to serve. 'You can't be what you can't see,' they say. I knew that I could try to influence policies or implement changes that could help ordinary people. But I didn't know that I would also be doing the hard work of trying to alter the mindsets of people and systems so entrenched in their biases. I had not envisaged complaining about an MP using the N-word or MPs telling me I didn't belong in Parliament

Some of the incidents I reported are in the public domain and common knowledge now, including a moment in 2006, when I was just a year into being the MP for Brent South. I was taking my staff out for lunch on the terrace in Parliament, which overlooks the Thames, when an MP physically tried to stop me. 'What are you doing here?' he asked. 'This is for members only. Are you a member?'

'Yes, I am. Are you?' With that, we went to sit down.

At this point, he turned to his guest and said something like, 'I don't believe her.'

I remember my staff being very upset, but my tolerance level for abuse is quite high. A bit like my parents when they arrived in the UK, I didn't have time to deal with every instance of prejudice and racism coming my way as a recently elected MP. It was a matter of self-preservation, and I wanted my team to have a good time. I remembered the advice that Paul Kenny had given me to pick my battles, so I wanted to walk away and get on with the rest of the day. But I could see how this situation was affecting my staff, and that they were having none of it. I decided that after lunch I would go back to the man.

I asked him why he thought he could speak to me in that manner. I could tell that this man of a certain generation just couldn't put together the image he saw in front of him with that of an MP. He was rude and dismissive. Shockingly, he said to me, 'They're letting anybody in nowadays,' then muttered that the place was going to 'rack and ruin'.

My staff and I demanded to know his name, but he refused to say. We found him in the end, and it took a lot of work and investigative skill to go through a book of at least six hundred white MPs. He was (at the time) a senior Tory minister, David Heathcoat-Amory. In Parliament we have no HR department so I had to complain to the Tory chief whip, who ignored me. I felt I had to take it further, so I went to the press. When asked for comment in the *Guardian*, he said my accusations of racism were 'quite absurd' and added, 'What she is actually objecting to is that I didn't recognize her as a new MP. I simply asked her what she was doing at that end of the terrace, and they are quite sensitive about this kind of thing; they think that any kind of reprimand from anyone is racially motivated. The trouble is that feminism has trumped everything. We are a bit obsessed with getting more women in and I think genuinely broad-based politics is one that takes people from every social and religious group. But we are exaggeratedly courteous to anyone with a different skin colour, so the idea that anything I have said is racist is absurd.'[2]

His tone here is indicative of the hostility I was up against. First, he wanted to set the record 'straight' by telling the *Guardian* what I was 'objecting to' as if I didn't know myself. Then he used 'they' to refer to Black people in a way that smelt of ignorance and contempt. *Why should we be complaining?* is the underlying message. It must have been a shock for him to realize that a Black woman could be elected as an MP. He then complained about feminism because women are *also* the problem.

Would he have had the same level of audacity to try to bar me from entering a space if I had been a white man? Or would he just have smiled? If I had been a white woman, I wonder if he would have thought twice about his approach to try to block my path. To behave in such a way even if I hadn't been an MP was just bad manners, but this was the sort of behaviour that confronted me when I entered an environment that had literally been designed for white men. This was supposed to be the mother of all parliaments, the cornerstone of our democracy, and we are servants to the people of our country or so I'd thought. I had to ask myself who Parliament was operating for. In whose best interests? Who are those in positions of power really serving?

Almost a year after the terrace episode, there would be the infamous incident in the lift. Certain lifts in Parliament are labelled as priority for MPs, so when the division bell rings MPs will often take them to get quickly to where they need to be. While I was in the lift, alongside several other politicians, I could hear their discussion about how cleaners shouldn't be allowed to use the lift – it was obvious they were talking about me. I was vexed and said in a loud voice that being a cleaner was a respectable way to make a living, and that they were plain rude. I then announced that I was an MP and a minister, who most likely had a larger majority than theirs. In truth, what I really wanted to say was 'F*** off', but I had no time to process how it made me feel as I was focused on getting to my committee.

I have spoken about the incident in the lift many times, but it came back to cause even more trouble when I mentioned it in a column for the *Metro* on Black History Month in 2019. I posted the article on Twitter, and a Lib Dem staffer, Steve Wilson, did what many have done before him: he accused me of lying. In response to my article, he wrote, 'Sorry but this is just not true. I've worked in Parliament for 15 years and the lifts have always been for the use of everyone. Only time MPs have priority is during a division. Stories like this don't do anyone any justice and anyone propagating then [*sic*] should stop it.'[3]

What possessed him to try to take me down a peg or two, I don't know. If he didn't believe me, he could have investigated, and it just seemed that he wanted to use his white male privilege to get people to attack me on social media. In response, I took a picture of the lifts that said, 'For MPs only'. Soon after that, I demanded (and received) an apology, writing to his wife, former Labour MP for Penistone and Stocksbridge, Angela Smith, whom he worked for, and the leader of the Liberal Democrats, Jo Swinson. I didn't have to take that picture but, as with the police incident, I thought evidence would be helpful. I wanted to defend myself against bullying and lies. I

shouldn't have to do this repeatedly – my lived experience of racism should be enough – but to change the
world we need to highlight discrimination continually
and take people through it step by step. Racial discrimination has been five hundred years in the making, and it's
going to take a while to undo.

The thing is, some people, especially those with certain
privilege, will try to take down anyone they *perceive* to be
a threat to them. Since becoming an MP, I've noticed a
certain type of white man – who can't stand to see me in
a position of power, who can't stand that I'm outspoken –
will often try to attack me. They never allow me to forget
just how irritating they find me because of my race, gender and class. It's disturbing that they thrive on the abuse,
as if the agenda is to take me down.

Much of the abuse started when Prime Minister The-
resa May appointed Toby Young to the Office of Students.
Several people highlighted a long list of problematic
tweets Young had written in the past, which they argued
made him unsuitable for public office. I was deeply
opposed to his appointment, not just because of the cronyism and his friendship with Boris Johnson, who was
foreign secretary at the time (both men were past and
present editors of the *Spectator* magazine) but also because
those tweets were massively offensive. To persuade the
prime minister to reverse her decision, I made a heated
speech to the Commons in January 2018, quoting some of
his messages. There was plenty of evidence of his misogyny, including a comment about a former MP's breasts,

and another referring to attending gay clubs dressed as a woman to molest lesbians.[4]

The lack of due diligence behind his appointment was disgraceful, but frustratingly not atypical of the Tory Party. A day after my speech, he resigned due to compounding pressures. I don't regret the speech I made in the Commons that day, but it has contributed to me being a target for a group of particularly horrid white men of a certain age.

A couple of months later, Young resurfaced with an article in the *Spectator* about how I'd 'spoiled' one of the best days of his life. As the MP for Brent Central, I had been invited to attend a Queens Park Rangers football game on behalf of their 'QPR in the community' campaign, where I was asked to hand out trophies to honour five 'local heroes' during half-time. One of those heroes happened to be Young's ten-year-old son, who had helped raise money for the survivors of the Grenfell tower block fire. To see me in person after what had happened was clearly very annoying for Young. According to his article, he first clocked me at the club restaurant. He writes, 'But just as I was beginning to enjoy myself, I spotted another guest at a neighbouring table: Dawn Butler. For those of you that don't know, Dawn is the Labour MP for Brent and the Shadow Secretary of State for Women and Equalities. She was also extremely rude about me in the House of Commons and on *Question Time* at the beginning of the year. [. . .] My plan was to stroll out on to the pitch with Freddie and bask in reflected glory, but I had no wish to be photographed with Dawn. I dare say she wasn't that keen to be pictured with me, either, and even if I swallowed my pride and went through with it, there was a risk she'd cause a scene. Disaster! So, I stopped at the edge of the tunnel and sent Freddie out on his own.'[5]

Toby Young needn't have worried as I am a professional and would never have caused a scene. Why would he have thought I'd suddenly go crazy? Was it because of the abuse he'd piled on me, or was it because he wasn't used to being told 'no' when his powerful friends had paved the way for him? It's funny how guilt presents itself: often people think that others will treat them in the way those others have been treated, but most of us who have been mistreated just want a better, fairer world, not revenge. If anyone is in any doubt, I would have shaken Young's hand and complimented the good work his son had done.

That summer, Young emerged again, not in person but in an article in the *Spectator*, defending Jamie Oliver after I'd called him out on Twitter for cultural appropriation. He'd launched a product called 'Punchy Jerk Rice' – a microwavable meal lacking the key ingredients relating to jerk, which is normally a marinade rubbed into meat. A traditional jerk chicken, for example, is cooked over pimento wood, and gets its recognizable flavour from spices native to Jamaica, such as allspice, ginger, garlic, thyme and Scotch bonnet peppers, which give the chicken that spicy kick. Other flavourings might include cloves, cinnamon, nutmeg, brown sugar, soy sauce and spring onions.

Yet again, here was a ploy to make money off the back of Jamaica and its culture. It felt exploitative, hit too close to home and simply got on my nerves. I tweeted, 'I'm just wondering do you know what #Jamaican #jerk actually is? It's not just a word you put before stuff to sell products [. . .] Your jerk rice is not OK. This appropriation from Jamaica needs to stop.'[6] I didn't expect it to blow up in the way it did, both on social media and the news. Some people came to Jamie Oliver's defence. I understand that chefs take inspiration from all kinds of cuisine, but I drew the line at calling something 'jerk' without paying homage to the authentic recipe – in that case, you might as well call the product something else entirely. When one of Oliver's famous chef friends wrote to ask why I didn't criticize Tilda's Jerk Rice, I wrote back to say that Tilda's at least had included the ingredients of 'Jerk herb and spice mix'. So much is appropriated from Jamaica, yet the country never gets the credit, or the financial benefits that come with it. Jamaica now takes the protection of geographical indicators (GI) seriously, and in 2018 it modified its laws. Jamaican Jerk is now a GI-protected term, rather like 'Champagne'.

Why did Toby Young feel the need to defend Jamie Oliver on a topic he had had nothing to do with? I feel I broke the flow for the privileged and well-connected and they didn't like it. And I'm not alone. We have seen relentless bullying from a particular sort of white man who takes to the media to belittle Black women with impunity. The level of racism and abuse that Meghan Markle received for marrying into the Royal Family is probably the foremost example in our minds. It wasn't just one or two white men who developed a troubling obsession with her, but news outlets as well, which continue to capitalize on hateful and bigoted articles against her.

I'm accustomed to this weird and perverted kind of obsession and was intrigued to discover that there was a word for the misogyny that Black women face on account of their race and gender: *misogynoir*. The word was coined by African American feminist and critical race scholar, Moya Bailey, and speaks to the intersection between our race and our gender that seems to make Black women more prone to attack by this gang of white men, who view us as easy prey, undeserving of care or respect, regardless of whether we critique them or not.

There is nothing I can do to ease the discomfort of my presence in systems previously built for white men. Nor would I want to. At the end of the day, my constituents elected me – they decided I belonged in Westminster. Whether or not these men see that as legitimate is of no concern to me. Every year, I give myself a goal of expanding on a theme I create as a talking point for my visits to schools in Brent and beyond – a few years ago it was to 'accept your greatness'. As a Black woman, I was constantly told I'd have to be twice as good to succeed. Therefore I say we should own it and understand that when we walk into a hostile room, we are already twice as good as most people there. Rather than changing ourselves to fit in, we should straighten our shoulders and walk tall, so we don't lose our crown, which, as Maya Angelou said, has already been paid for by those on whose shoulders we stand.

No one, no matter their skin colour, sexuality, religion or gender identity, should have to ease the discomfort of their presence in a rigid and unimaginative system, especially when they have worked so hard to get there. You will always encounter people with a self-inflated view of themselves and their worth, who expect everyone else to prove they belong in a space they think was made for them. And I suppose, at one time or another, those spaces *were* made for them. But the world is changing, expanding and waking up to the reality that these illusions of superiority and privilege are false and destructive. For some of these men there's a deep-seated fear behind the hostility. A fear that people like me – a Black woman – are attempting to take away their power and privilege. *This is the way things have always been done, so let it be.* They are fixed in their ways and want to continue to dominate and control. They feel themselves beyond change or transformation. If you call them racist, you're blowing things out of proportion, race-baiting, troublesome, or you have a chip on your shoulder. If you complain of sexism, you're a prude or you have no sense of humour.

Unfortunately these people often aren't that good at their jobs but are promoted anyway because of their privilege and connection. A fair way of doing things isn't beneficial to them. The fear comes from the realization that they potentially have to relinquish control.

Once we change the system, everything else changes. Once people are promoted on their ability to do a job, not on how well they down a pint at the pub (a big generalization, but you get what I mean), the top of an organization will look different and act differently.

Another previous theme was around careers, using the imagery of the escalator and the lift. The traditional career ladder is the old-fashioned way of promotion where every rung to the promotion goal is filled with a problem or a favour – for women it could be ignoring a sexist remark or a touch on the leg so you won't ruin your chances of promotion. An escalator shows you progressing up the ranks by doing your job well and the system automatically recognizing that. And then there's the lift, which is how the accidental managers get to the top – *the ones who really shouldn't be there.* They're given the code by the old boys' club, therefore advancing to the top without necessarily earning it. Those are the people most scared by a change of the system, who will try to keep stereotypes alive because anything else will expose their incapability. They need to have people around them who will defend them and their ways – why embrace progress, when they have things so cushy? All organizations should aspire to the escalator model, in my opinion.

We can no longer afford to operate within systems that only serve a particular person or class. They don't function well for an ever-changing society with a multi-tude of issues that need to be urgently addressed. If we could work to create systems that benefit everyone, and that incorporate a wide variety of people reflective of the society that we are living in, the world would truly be a safer and more productive place. There would be more approaches to consider and more unique viewpoints to incorporate instead of the same old staleness that we are constantly encountering. None of what I'm saying is new. It's just that the people operating the systems and struc-tures that govern our lives fail to change, and they are continually getting us into the mess we are now in.

*

I rarely told my family about the discrimination I faced at work because I knew how angry they would be for me. On one occasion, I'd gone campaigning with my family when my sister had an argument with a woman because she said something negative about me. My brother came running when he heard someone shouting at me. Man-aging their expectations of how I can be treated is hard – but there are brilliant times around election days. My brothers like to pick up the elderly and drive them to the polling stations while having a nice chat. It's their favourite thing to do, as they're used to working with older people in their day jobs. Donald fits equipment for people who are disabled to ensure they can live more independently, and Owen fits double-glazed windows.

(He also ends up putting up a lot of curtain rails for his older customers!) Time with my family is always a chance to put work aside, to enjoy the nicer things in life, like food and laughter, but sometimes work and family collide, with interesting results.

A few years back, my dad became confused as to why I wasn't quickly made a minister. In his (obviously biased) opinion, I was a good communicator, and he wanted to know why the Labour Party were missing a trick. Without telling me, my dad got my cousin to write a letter to Gordon Brown telling him he should make me a minister. Years later I was *mortified* when I found out. My dad was always there for me during my school days, but I'd come to a point in my life when I had to say, 'It's okay, Dad, I'm an adult now. I have my own words. I can fight my own battles.' Eventually I was promoted, but not because of Dad's letter.

As Gordon Brown's minister, I helped prepare him for Prime Minister's Questions. One afternoon, we rehearsed together in his office in the House of Commons, and with a few minutes to spare, I rushed to see a visitor in the Pugin Room (a posh tearoom in the Commons) before PMQs began. On my way in, a police officer stopped me and asked where I was going. He demanded to see my pass, but in my hurry, I'd left it in the prime minister's office. I was very apologetic and the staff who worked in the tearoom all vouched for me. They told him that I was Dawn Butler, an MP and government minister, but the officer refused to let me in.

'I've literally got five minutes,' I said. 'I need to say hello to this person before I go back to the prime minister who's waiting for me.' But that didn't ease the officer's approach. Instead he responded aggressively before following me inside to greet my guest, standing over me as if I were a criminal. The tearoom staff were up in arms. If he wanted verification that I was an MP, he could look at the book that contained pictures of sitting MPs in Parliament, but he refused. It soon became clear that he had a personal issue with me, and that, in turn, he needed to assert his power. When I left the room, I asked for his police number, but he hid it from me. It took another officer to give me his details before I could make an official complaint.

I soon received another letter of apology. One of many I have in a drawer. Like all the others it was only a formality. I knew how much the officer had enjoyed abusing his power that day, even if he had apologized for being 'slightly overzealous' and for causing me 'stress and embarrassment'. The point was that he had wanted to intimidate me, put me in my place, just like the officers who had surrounded my friend and me in the car, or the MPs in the lift, and the many other times I have yet to mention. Some people take joy from putting others down, and they should be nowhere near power.

I am constantly coming up against people who want me to leave the racism argument behind. *Why do you have to keep talking about it? Why are you race-baiting?* Even if I wanted to leave this discussion behind, I can't! The reminder is there for me every single day. All it takes is one look at the type of emails that come into my inbox daily. Or a scroll through my Twitter feed. I wish it was the case that racism and sexism didn't exist, but we aren't going to get to that stage by wishing and sweeping it under the rug. Even though I'm not afraid to discuss the subject matter, it shouldn't be my sole responsibility to teach people about racism – it exists, therefore people need to take an active role in eradicating it.

Many people are still scared when you talk about oppression from a Black perspective: it seems threatening and churns up feelings of guilt, denial and discomfort that people don't want to admit to or don't know how to push through. When I talk about race in predominantly white spaces, I often reference my arguments from a woman's perspective first because it seems to resonate more with people and is more comfortable to them. Once I've established that parallel of oppression, I find it easier to expand to race – that is how deep the guilt and discomfort run.

It is not always about the colour or heritage of the person. That same discomfort impacts some of my Black colleagues as well, particularly those who have tried to discredit my experiences of racism as if to make their white colleagues more comfortable or to profit from the alignment of white privilege. It seems they have assessed that if they assimilate into the existing system, they'll benefit by being promoted. Not every Black person has the same lived experience, but for another Black politician to say that racism doesn't exist is beyond me. They may have been fortunate enough to go through life without any racist experiences – and good for them, if that's the case (perhaps their class has helped smooth their path) – but that doesn't mean every other Black person has been unscathed. Denying racism makes things even more difficult for those of us who have suffered it, or who are trying to change the system to address it. It pits Black people against each other in a predominantly white space, so that white politicians feel at liberty to say, 'Oh, so and so said racism doesn't exist. You must be lying.' (The same goes for sexism: women who are embarrassed by the #MeToo Movement shock me because that pits women against women.) If one Black politician wants to say racism doesn't exist that is their prerogative, but it doesn't mean their opinion is fact.

When you're tackling a problem, you cannot give equal weight to the lived experience of someone who has apparently never been subject to racism and that of a person who has. Imagine you have two women in front of you: one has suffered domestic violence and the other has only ever had wonderful relationships with men. Would you believe the latter if she said domestic violence didn't exist? Would you believe her rather than the woman who has been bruised and broken? That is exactly what happens in the racism 'debate', which I find baffling. More open and honest conversations are required from all of us. We should be unafraid to call out the truth of a situation and discuss it (perhaps even bringing in mediation), so that real and effective progress can take shape. Unfortunately, this requires us to be massively uncomfortable, but we cannot afford to stay silent or leave it to somebody else to sort out. We must all play our part, which does not encompass only racism, but sexism, homophobia, misogyny and transphobia too.

Those early knockbacks of racism and sexism in Parliament were prominent in my career, but so were the moments worth celebrating. Towards the tail end of 2009, I became the first African-Caribbean woman to speak as a government minister at the House of Commons despatch box. Boy, was I nervous – beyond nervous, if the truth be told. But I was comforted by the fact that I knew my brief inside out and was very much prepared. Before my departmental questions, Sadiq Khan, MP for Tooting at the time, called to ask what time I was going into the chamber. When I told him I was on my way, he shouted, 'WHAT?' and ran from the other side of Parliament to sit next to me. 'You're about to make history, and you didn't tell me!' he reprimanded.

Sadiq wanted to know if I had flagged my historical achievement to the first person asking a question, so they could reference the moment and have it recorded in Hansard in perpetuity. (Hansard holds the transcripts of all Parliamentary debates.) I shook my head. All I could focus on was making sure I did well, that I didn't mess up, because if I did, I knew everyone would be talking (or thinking) about the Black woman who messed up. Sadiq said to the first speaker, 'Dawn Butler is the first

Black woman to talk at this despatch box. Don't forget to mention it.' Later, there were cheers, I think, from both sides.

If Sadiq hadn't been there to make a fuss, and to elevate my moment, I wouldn't have done so. It felt good to have someone there to remind me that I was doing something phenomenal and historic. There was no shortage of people waiting to catch me out if I made a mistake.

I never needed to find my detractors because they gravitated towards me like flies. Case in point, four months later during another debate, I had handled all the questions coming my way, but this was obviously too much for some of the Tories on the other side of the room. One of them stood up and said, 'Will the Minister very kindly stop this assault on the English language? Can we drop these awful terms, such as "upskilling" and "third sector"?' I thought, *What a f****** prick* – it was such an obvious move to try to belittle me, and to make sure that I didn't feel good enough. I told him that 'upskilling' was now a recognized and understandable term. 'I apologize if the Honourable Gentleman is put off by it,'[7] I said, and explained the meaning of the word (which anyone can google).

What has got me through my time in Parliament is the knowledge that I have friends, who support and understand me, and Sadiq has been one of those people. I will never forget him running from one side of the House to the other to sit with me in my history-making moment – a moment that might easily have been unacknowledged.

I believe it's important to acknowledge our firsts, not only because it's a phenomenal thing to do – we should all be bigging ourselves up and reminding ourselves of our accomplishments – but also because as a woman, and especially a Black woman, it's not uncommon for my achievements, along with those of others, to be ignored, downplayed or erased from history. I asked my office to get a list of firsts in Parliament from the House of Commons library and, to my surprise, I was not on it. That is how easy it would have been for my achievements to be missed. Thankfully, the library corrected it straight away.

In life, it is of fundamental importance to surround yourself with people who will go the extra mile for you, people who are givers, not just takers, people you can rely on for honest feedback, who will never be jealous of your achievements. Instead, they will elevate you. They say that you never make friends in politics, but my friendship with Sadiq bucks that trend. He does a great job, and it's one that I would love to do. I hope that one day I will be able to follow in his footsteps as Mayor of London.

6

WE ARE PHENOMENAL WOMEN

THERE WILL ALWAYS BE THOSE who want to uphold the status quo and others who want to dismantle it. But it's more disappointing when those divisions appear between women. I had no awareness of the term 'white feminism' until I read about it a few years ago. It was reassuring to have a term to describe how I felt as a Black female MP among some of my white female colleagues. The examples of our divisions, and the power dynamics inherent within them, were small but frustrating.

When I was complaining to a senior white female MP about the instances of racism I experienced in Parliament, she replied, 'Well, at least they weren't talking about your tits.' Instead of a compassionate or even empathetic response, as I would have hoped and expected, her words seemed to suggest . . . Well, I'm not sure what her words were suggesting: that it would've been preferable for men to be talking about my tits? Or that male MPs had talked about hers or the tits of other women and that was somehow worse? Or that I had it better because even though I had tits, they weren't talking about them and instead, thank God, were focusing on the fact that I was Black? It felt like a competition to see who had it worse, instead of trying to address the root of the problem. And the general point seemed to be that I should get over the racism (or the sexism) and move on.

After a string of comments like this from women I'd thought would be natural allies, it became clear to me that trying to fit into Parliament was going to be hard work.

Most of us will agree that overt racism and sexism are shocking, but instances of unconscious bias often get swept under the rug. This is behaviour I find more troubling in its commonality and subtlety. Putting myself on the firing line to call someone out on bias isn't something I want to do, because it's draining to raise it, but when it affects my ability to do my job or to live a happy life, I most definitely will say something. I can't always predict how the situation will unfold – no one likes to be told that they're behaving wrongly or unjustly. All I know is that I must air my feelings if things are to change. I speak up to smooth the path for others to follow. I'm always surprised when I'm thanked for raising an issue or standing up to an injustice. I don't do it for thanks, but the acknowledgement helps to recharge my batteries so I can continue the fight. I hope that the conversations I will have through this book will help others along their journey.

The nerdy side of me loves being a member of House of Commons committees as we delve into critical and wide-ranging issues. The committees exist to investigate specific areas of interest and to hold the government to account, calling in ministers and external experts in particular fields. As members of a committee, we are each given a chance by the chair to question the invited speakers. But during my time on the Commons Science and Technology Committee, I often found that whenever it was my turn to ask a question, I wouldn't be given much time to speak. I wasn't sure if the disparity in time I was allowed in comparison to other members was fact or feeling (a bit of paranoia kicked in), so I needed to test my theory before voicing my concerns. I started timing the length of people's questions, noticing that the chair might spend half an hour drilling down on the initial opening, with the next person having about twenty minutes, and the person after that maybe ten minutes. By the time it got to me, I'd have about three minutes to get across my points and questions. That wasn't enough to set the scene and interrogate someone, especially at crucial moments during the pandemic, when I might be questioning Matt Hancock over PPE.

Overall, women tended to speak later, so it appeared that the women on the committee were being short-changed. I even had people email me about this. I'd approached another woman in the group who revealed she felt the same, and eventually we raised the issue in committee, with a suggestion that we rotate so that the women weren't always left until last. The result was that we were given a little more equality in time. The Science and Technology Committee is one of the best committees I have sat on. Members from each of the political parties bring their expertise and experience to the table so we are in constant learning mode, and we are often formidable as a group. It's politics at its best.

Sometimes tackling unconscious bias isn't resolved so smoothly. In 2015, it became clear to me and a few other MPs of colour that racial bias was negatively impacting our debates. To make a speech, MPs contact the Speaker's Office to add their names to a list before debates. That's not to say that allowances can't be made for names to be squeezed on during debates, but this is typical protocol. Quite a few of my Black and Asian colleagues noticed that we were being called late or not at all, while our white colleagues were called often and early. This might not sound like a big deal but when you're sitting in the chamber for eight hours and there are more than ten MPs ahead of you, it's not exactly comfortable. There seemed to be a lack of a fair rotation, and the frustration of my colleagues of colour grew until they lodged formal complaints.

My neighbouring MP, Tulip Siddiq of Hampstead and Kilburn, was heavily pregnant when she waited around two hours to speak in 2016. After she'd finally spoken, she left the chamber to go to the loo and to have something to eat as she was feeling faint. Parliamentary protocol is that you wait for the two members following you to speak before leaving the chamber. So, in response to Tulip's departure, the Conservative deputy speaker

Eleanor Laing told Tulip that she 'made women look bad', scolding her, not to 'play the pregnancy card.'[1] In what other workplace would such treatment be accepted? During a housing debate, my patience wore thin, and after waiting for quite a long time to speak, I approached the deputy speaker to enquire about my place on the list. I was given an indication, saw my name on the list, and went back to my seat to wait. I wondered whether I had time to rush to the loo, and decided I could wait the twenty minutes or so. But as time passed, and the deputy speaker changed (the length of parliamentary debates requires that each speaker do a certain number of hours), I still hadn't been called, and by this point I was bursting.

I approached the new deputy speaker, Eleanor Laing, and asked how long I'd wait to be called. Her answer totally floored me. According to her, I wasn't on the list. This confused me as the previous deputy had said otherwise, and Eleanor wasn't to know that I had previously seen my name, so for her to say that was astounding. My hours of waiting to be called had been for nothing. I was wasting my time in the chamber when I could have been in another meeting or back at my desk. I went to walk away, then thought better of it and told her I had seen my name. She backtracked, this time saying I would not be called because I'd been called so many times in so many different debates. *Really?* As far as I was concerned, I was hardly ever called, and now I was irritated. This wasn't something I was about to let go, because I wasn't the only one affected. Many of my colleagues also suffered from this bias, which was directly affecting our ability to do our jobs. I told her I thought she had a racial bias in her decision-making because it was obvious that MPs of colour were being short-changed.

When the deputy speaker mentioned that I had spoken too many times in different debates, the reality was that I had *intervened* twice that year and had made one speech. When we later exchanged letters about the matter, she mentioned that I had given up to three speeches that year. She believed I had given many speeches because she remembered me talking or being impassioned, thus taking up a lot of space. Therefore, I needed to speak last or not at all. To the deputy speaker, it was as if I had spoken yesterday instead of a month ago. Her bias had a profound effect on my ability to carry out the rest of my responsibilities: I spent so much time in the chamber waiting to be called that I was prevented from doing other parts of my job.

The ultimate result was that, to protect my mental health, I would avoid the chamber if she was in the chair. But how many times does a person have to adjust their behaviour to avoid conflict or discrimination? We all have to prioritize our wellbeing and make the appropriate decisions to do so, and sometimes we need to make conscious adjustments to protect ourselves, but why should people have to adjust their reasonable behaviour to appease the perpetrator? We should not have to exist in a workplace or a society where some people remain comfortable while others are kept voiceless and disenfranchised. As a

Black woman, I am used to being invisible or overlooked, mistaken for a member of the service staff or an MP's assistant rather than the MP. But when it suits the system, I can also be hyper-visible. In that moment my outspokenness (a key part of my job as an MP) counted against me. Even if I *had* given three speeches, how could that be considered too many?

After the incident, I wrote a formal letter of complaint to the deputy speaker, but before I received the speaker's response, it mysteriously found its way to the press. What caught me off guard was that even though I never received a copy of this letter, all blame – via the tabloid press – fell on me. Funny, isn't it, that when you challenge the system, it fights back to protect the status quo? The situation blew up, with a handful of articles published in the right-wing papers that tried to paint all Black and Asian MPs as forever moaning. The deputy speaker became upset with me for allegedly calling her a 'racist' and claimed others were questioning my challenge too, including, she said, her son, who had become privy to the news. In one of her letters, she told me she had always been an advocate for equality and she didn't have a racist bone in her body. But the whole point of the matter is that a lot of these behaviours – which are not unique to her – are deeply ingrained and only show up in ways that are imperceptible to the perpetrator.

I did not call her a racist, but I have often said that when accused of bias or racism, there are three things you should never respond with:

1. 'I haven't got a racist bone in my body.' Racism doesn't exist in your bones, it exists in your mind, in the amygdala.[2]
2. 'I have a Black friend.' Having a Black friend is not your get-out-of-racist-jail-free card.
3. 'I don't see colour.' It is wrong to say that you don't see differences as it dismisses people's experiences and, quite frankly, it's offensive – I am happy being an African-Caribbean woman. To say you don't see differences doesn't help the fight against racism.

To resolve the situation as best we could and come to an understanding, a programme of unconscious bias interventions was proposed between the deputy speaker and myself, which was mediated by Naz Shah, MP. The sessions involved a lot of time, a lot of patience, and a lot of discomfort, but sometimes being uncomfortable is a good indicator that you are learning or unlearning behaviour.

Unconscious bias is hard for some people to grasp or even admit to because of its subtlety. Unless you're doing the hard work of constantly identifying your biases, they won't be apparent to you, and you won't know how or when they formed your opinions and behaviours. These days, especially in the workplace, there are repercussions for being overtly racist, but more covert biases get swept under the carpet. As a Black woman working in predominantly white spaces, I find unconscious bias can be subtle to the point at which even I am asking myself why, and is this really happening? Am I making a fuss about nothing? So much shame and confusion are wrapped around the admission of such behaviour that some will make you feel you are constantly overreacting. Trust me, you're not. If you feel something is not right and you have the strength to do so, address it. Maybe the person is oblivious to the damage their actions are causing, and your intervention will help.

Bias manifests in so many ways, and each time it does, I'm expected to be quiet or even lenient, despite repeated harm. When I'm mistaken for Diane Abbott, Marsha de Cordova, Bell Ribeiro-Addy, Florence Eshalomi, Abena Oppong-Asare or any other Black woman in Parliament, it's not only clichéd but exhausting to be reminded of just how invisible Black women can be. I've often called my good friend and mentor Dawn Airey, who has worked for Getty Images, Channel 5, ITV and Sky, and we get angry about this situation together. I don't have enough fingers to count how many times journalists, for example, have mistaken us, despite our differences in hairstyles, skin colours and body types. It has also happened several times on TV where we have each been given the name caption of another Black woman. If it weren't so tragic, I'd have to laugh (and sometimes my comrades and I do because of the sheer stupidity of it all). Think how many white men exist in Parliament – more than half of 650 MPs – yet how rarely they are mistaken for one another. Instead, they are given the dignity and respect they seem to be systemically entitled to having. As a Black MP, I talk about these issues not because I want to, but because I can't escape them, and if I can't escape them, I have to talk about them until change happens.

But how can we practically make that change? Would journalists be so reckless as to make assumptions about the identity of a white male Tory MP? Or is this lack of care and attention reserved for people of colour? If there are no Black people in a newsroom or in publishing, for example, silly mistakes such as misidentification are more likely to happen. We need to diversify our institutions to reflect our society. More and more Black female MPs are coming into Parliament, and I believe that if I don't speak up and point out unconscious bias, or campaign for change across the media, they will struggle to be known by their own names or be given their own identities for the work they do. They should be known as individuals, as they have worked so hard to get to Westminster.

You can tell a lot about a person when push comes to shove and they're asked to examine their unconscious beliefs and how they affect their thoughts and behaviours. Some people think they're beyond learning and would rather cling to the familiarity of their egos. They fail to accept that they can see the world only through their own lens, and that someone else – a woman, a person of colour, a disabled person, an LGBTQI+ person – will be seeing it through a different lens and set of experiences.

We are all born with different privileges, which may include skin colour, sight, hearing, ability, height or sex, and we will navigate our world through our privilege.

Certain privileges will be afforded to a white person without them asking for or noticing them. If you are a young white boy, for example, you are less likely to be stopped and searched by the police. At school I remember my white friend saying she liked going into the shop with me because I was her decoy: security was so busy watching me that she could do whatever she pleased. I have heard the same story even as recently as 2022.

Those who are willing to admit that their view of the world has been limited, and those who are curious, and care about others, and who have empathy for other people's lived experiences will be open to engaging in difficult conversations and changing. Not everyone will want to and that's their prerogative, but for those who do, I'll say that it requires a lot of hard work. If we can become aware of our biases and interrogate where they come from, then have the willingness to do better, our relationships with colleagues, neighbours and strangers will feel more harmonious. We can strengthen our communities and workplaces, and pave the way for more people to break through. We can learn so much by educating ourselves, through reading books or articles or listening to podcasts, for example. But this requires that we put aside our guilt, shame and denial, and do what we must to see others in a more dignified light.

In some cases, it takes something dramatic or personal to confront our biases. When I was a magistrate, the chair, a white man, thought that all Black men were criminals. I'm oversimplifying things but that's how it felt – the only Black men he encountered were those in front of him waiting to be sentenced so he believed that all Black men must be cut from the same cloth. Then his daughter married a Black man and had a baby, his first grandchild. He changed. He wouldn't stop banging on about how his son-in-law had a good job and was such a good man. Although it grated on me a little, I was pleased that the love of his grandchild and his Black son-in-law made him see young Black men in a different light.

It shouldn't take family ties, money or status to empathize with a person who is different from you. In many cases, breaking down our biases requires us to form relationships with those who are radically different. This shouldn't be forced. Sometimes it will happen naturally, but it helps if we keep an open mind about the people around us, even if they might seem 'different'. After all, at the end of the day we are all one human race.

*

I had thought that women were all in the feminist fight together. I quickly learned that that is not always the case: issues that were important to my white female colleagues often took precedence over other, equally pressing, concerns. It was hard to reconcile my feminism with what I witnessed when the issues I brought to the table, which affected the most marginalized and forgotten, were cold-shouldered, and never seen as a priority.

In 2018, MPs began a debate about the need for proxy

votes in the House of Commons, a scheme that would enable them to vote on behalf of another under special circumstances. The conversation centred around proxy votes for new mothers (and later new fathers) and those experiencing childbirth complications or caring for an infant/newly adopted child. The Women's PLP – a sub-group of the Parliamentary Labour Party (PLP) which I'll get to in a bit – discussed this during a weekly meeting.

There were a couple of pregnant MPs in the room, so the issue was understandably very important to them, but I suggested we extend these rights to those who had cancer, for instance, or were in hospital. I was immediately shut down, told we should focus on new mothers first, then essentially come back for everyone else. This was exactly what had happened when women first campaigned for the right to vote, I pointed out, with working-class women being left behind. I thought we had all learned from that. I was supported by another MP who had previously had cancer, but she backed down when the rest of the room shot her a look.

Despite her personal reasons for supporting the expanded scope of the proxy vote, she felt it was too difficult to go against the grain of this matriarchy of very important white women, who made it clear that there would be no room for debate or discussion. In my mind, it made sense for us to expand the parameters of those who might benefit from the proxy votes as soon as possible, instead of creating false hierarchies as to who was most important. It took until 2022 for the votes to be extended to those suffering serious long-term illness or injury. (This was initially rolled out as a pilot scheme. At the time of writing, the Commons Procedure Committee report concluded that the illness and injury proxy voting pilot has been a success, and the extension of eligibility should be made on a permanent basis, subject to certain amendments made to the scheme issued by the speaker.)

What struck me most in that moment was the lack of care for other people's experiences and the inability to see how we all intersected. Is it really that difficult to make our policies inclusive so that they benefit as many people as possible initially? I've found white feminism often fails to consider the lived experiences of women of colour, or other marginalized women. It hardly considers how these experiences might differ from its own, thus creating a hierarchy of which are the issues that matter. To continue in this way slows progress in the fight for equity. If you take universal suffrage, for example, married women were allowed to vote first, but it took a further ten years before working-class women were given the vote. And they only came after working-class men!

Feminism should include and be informed by a range of voices and opinions, and it should be able to take on board the wealth of lived experiences that exist between women. I appreciate that it is unrealistic to have unity between people all the time. When you have a large group of people coming together, there will be disagreements, and the hope is that they can be dealt with appropriately.

When I became the first Black female chair of the

Women's PLP in 2015, I was thrilled and looked forward to tackling some big issues with the support of everyone: I like to think I am not factional in my internal politics. The PLP consists of all the Labour MPs within the party, with the Women's PLP a sub-group, created in 1992 by Jean Corston and Helen Jackson, the inaugural chairs (but they were not MPs). Lorna Fitzsimmons became the first MP to chair between 1997 and 2001, and most chairs stayed for roughly two years.

We came together weekly to discuss pending legislation and all things politics, but for me there had always been something quite cliquey about the meetings. So, as the new chair, I sought to make our meetings more inclusive, transparent, and more of a safe space where we could all speak about our goals and ambitions as a collective. I wanted the female MPs in attendance to feel relaxed and looked after, so I introduced sandwiches and snacks during our lunchtime meetings – I knew how easy it was to forget to eat when we were all so busy. This was a hit.

As the attendance grew, we worked well together as a group. I was proud of my chairing skills as I had worked to improve them over many years. I often say it is my USP.

The beginning of my time as chair went smoothly and the women's PLP felt open, a place where we treated one another with respect. But around September 2015, when Jeremy Corbyn became leader of the Labour Party, things began to change.

Suddenly, within the Women's PLP, a group of women

tried, it seemed, to use our weekly meetings as a forum to attack and criticize the leader. It almost felt like meetings were organized prior to our Women's PLP meetings where these women would prepare attack lines, which they'd then fire off. As a woman who prides herself on her fairness, I wanted them to unpack their complaints and talk through their issues with Jeremy. I even suggested that we invite him to a meeting so that he could answer questions himself and address their concerns. But someone objected to this, instead wanting to send a press statement signed by the Women's PLP. There were women in the meeting texting me about how uncomfortable they felt but also how reluctant they were to speak up. In the end there was no evidence to support a statement that Jeremy was misogynistic. In fact, the majority of his shadow cabinet were women, and he had more women of colour than any other leader.

At times this unrelenting focus on Jeremy made my job of chairing more difficult than it needed to be, but ultimately we were achieving positive outcomes as a group. If I had learned anything during the proxy-vote meeting, it was that some women can be rigid in their views. I refused to take this to heart because I had a job to do and, by all measures, I seemed to be doing it well.

The situation came to a head during the summer of 2016. I don't know who was responsible for the request, but I was asked to produce a report collating everything I had done as chair to date. To my knowledge, this was the first time in the history of the Women's PLP that a chair had been asked to do such a thing. And what was a report supposed to prove exactly? The played-out racial stereotype of laziness? As a Black woman, I am no stranger to hurdles appearing out of nowhere and having to go the extra mile to prove myself, but this assignment felt like a slap in the face.

I told my staff member Lee to go to town on it, and he produced an eleven-page document, double-sided. It included things like advocating for women in the party directly with the leader and deputy leader across a range of issues such as culture, protecting women in upcoming boundary changes and pushing for an enhanced level of involvement in policy-making. I lobbied the Labour Party over the need for organizational and structural change, specifically the need to create dedicated positions on the National Executive Committee (NEC) elected only by women in the party, and for an additional deputy/ chair of the party who should always be a woman, placing women at the core of party leadership.

I also worked with the then Procedure Committee chair to push for changes around the sitting hours of the House to make them more women-friendly, as well as working to deliver a Jo Cox award for women. This is just the tip of the iceberg.

By this point, I was ready to jack in the chair of the Women's PLP because I wasn't enjoying it. It was mentally affecting me. I had to psych myself up before every meeting, but when I spoke to another MP about stepping down, she asked me not to. I convinced myself I could continue for a little longer. But, unknown to me, a coup to remove me as chair, led by the MPs Harriet Harman and Jess Phillips, was in the offing. When a change of chair comes about, there's usually a conversation to agree a change and a civil handover. But those women had other ideas, and it took a whistle-blower to warn me and say, 'Dawn, they're coming for you . . . They're organizing against you.'

At that point, I could have stepped down as chair and saved myself the pain of going through an ambush, but I decided against it. I wanted to stand up and expose the unfairness of what was happening, but I was upset and needed to vent before the upcoming meeting for which I had little time to prepare.

I called Naz Shah, MP, who was just as shocked as I was. She could hear the feeling of having been betrayed in my voice and wanted to be there to support me, but she was on the road from Bradford, making her way to Westminster. She couldn't be there in person, but she assured me that she'd make some calls. I wanted and needed some friends and allies in the room and called a senior MP, with whom I'd served in government, to ask if she was also part of the coup. She promised she had no idea what was going on. I told her how disappointed I was that this was how I was being treated by a group of white female MPs. And that this was not my idea of feminism.

There were fake smiles and niceties at the meeting, although it felt more like an execution. I looked around the packed room and noticed a woman of advanced years from the House of Lords arrive on a zimmer frame. I only mention this detail because I had never seen her at a meeting before and, to be honest, it seemed like an inconvenience for her to be there. Her presence, along with that of many senior women from the House of Lords, felt like an additional layer of intimidation. I thought, *Wow, they really have gone through their address book to see who they could find to vote me out, when all they needed to do was ask.* I would gladly have stepped down.

Many women in the room hadn't realized they were part of a coup against me, but they soon understood. I could see in their faces how embarrassed they were, so much so that one woman stood to thank me for my work as chair. But I said, 'You don't get to thank me when you've come in to attack me.' It was important for me not to take the easy route and step down, because I needed some of the people in the room that day to feel deeply uncomfortable at their role in the ambush. They needed to witness the disgraceful behaviour of their colleagues and understand what had really happened.

I became closer to a few of those MPs later, who hadn't liked the nature of the coup, but had probably felt powerless to stop it. And I will always remember Caroline Adams, our amazing administrator, who is always completely neutral, but I could feel her positive vibes towards me from across the room. I think, if she could have, she would have given me a hug. It's tough to speak up against seniority at the cost of exclusion – after all, there is belonging, safety and ease in numbers. To change the hearts of some of those women, I had to sacrifice myself. As a result, they soon began taking the time to ask how I was or about my feelings – I'm sure part of this was out of guilt, but also, hopefully, a lesson learned in terms of compassion and feminism.

Jess Phillips, the newly elected MP of Birmingham Yardley, became the new chair. She rose to fame for allegedly telling Diane Abbott, the first Black female MP, to 'fuck off' during a parliamentary meeting. Although Diane denied this ever happened, Phillips bragged about her behaviour, and the newspapers ate it up. *Huffington Post UK* said, 'Ms Phillips, who despite being elected in May has already earned a reputation for being one of the most outspoken MPs, said: "I roundly told her to fuck off."

'When asked what Ms Abbott did after that suggestion, Ms Phillips replied: "She fucked off."

'She added: "People said to me they had always wanted to say that to her, and I don't know why they don't as the opportunity presents itself every other minute."'[3]

She was lauded for being outspoken, a 'breath of fresh air', but if the tables were turned and a newly elected Black female MP had told a senior white female MP to 'fuck off', it would have caused uproar and they would probably have been seen as any number of things – unprofessional, aggressive, a disgrace to the party and Parliament. These are the societal double standards that exist between white and Black women.

How regrettable then that Jess Phillips would work

hand in hand with the 'Mother of the House' to oust me, the first Black chair.[4] To this day I wonder why one of them couldn't have picked up the phone to speak with me. It was an AGM and it was customary that if someone wanted to challenge, they would have a discussion with the sitting chair, to either replace or chair jointly. No one has the entitlement to continue as chair, but the way my fellow parliamentarians treated me showed a lack of regard for my feelings, an utter disrespect for me or the great work I had done. The coup only reiterated that the voice and presence of all women is not always welcome.

I recall speaking to the writer and columnist Gary Younge, whom I consider the fountain of all knowledge, and he confirmed with me that what took place that day was white feminism at its worst. Politicians get away with this kind of behaviour because it requires those of us in the firing line to stay quiet for the greater good of the party or system. Some are expected to stay quiet while the voices of others are amplified – when it suits the system. The irony is that the only way to change the system is to highlight the issues and problems within it, and to examine our own behaviours when we are confronted by an uncomfortable truth.

As women, and as a society in general, we have to look out and advocate for each other, no matter our differences. We won't always like each other or agree with each other, but we should have the common decency to treat each other with respect, and to have open and honest conversations when problems arise. When faced with a moral dilemma, whether at work, in public, or in organizations, it's best to put aside our discomfort and to speak out, trusting that at least we did our part to achieve justice. It's better to sleep easy at night than to go to bed with a guilty conscience.

Under Corbyn's leadership, I became shadow secretary of state for women and equalities in the summer of 2017, and I spoke at Labour's National Women's Conference that year. Here was a chance to be involved in a conference to uplift women. Up to a thousand women from all over the country came together to engage in training sessions and policy debates around issues such as Brexit, the NHS, housing and the economy. The morning launched with speeches from myself, Emily Thornberry, MP, the shadow foreign secretary, and Jeremy Corbyn.

Some months before the conference, the worst fire in recent UK history had destroyed Grenfell Tower, a block in West London. Seventy-two lives were tragically lost, exposing massive inequalities in housing, so I opened my speech with a moment of silence for the victims. After this, I sensed that our energy needed lifting, and I asked the women in the room to repeat after me, 'We are phenomenal women', evoking lines from one of my favourite poems, 'Phenomenal Woman', by Maya Angelou. Each time my hand rose throughout my speech, the audience – full of MPs, councillors, activists and volunteers – would repeat it after me.

My speech touched on how racism and sexism had featured heavily in my journey as an MP, and how as a result I aimed to continue tackling all the injustices within my new role. I spoke of intersectionality, a term that refers to how some people face discrimination across multiple identities (including gender, sexuality, race and class), and stressed the saying, 'United we stand. Divided we fall,' which spoke to what the trade unions had taught me. I talked about spearheading the period-poverty campaign in Britain, an initiative the Scottish Labour MSP, Monica Lennon, had inspired me to undertake after she tabled her excellent Bill. The goal was to make period products not just affordable but free, as the most vulnerable in society (homeless women, women on low incomes) couldn't afford them. At the time it was estimated that women spent around £5,000 in their lifetime on sanitary products. We pledged to provide funding for free sanitary products for secondary schools, food banks and homeless shelters.

I closed my speech with an adaptation of Angelou's poem. Instead of reciting her first line, 'Pretty women wonder where my secret lies', I said, '*Privileged* women wonder where my secret lies, I'm not built to a size-ten supermodel size, but when I start to tell them, they think I'm telling lies, I say it's in the reach of my arms, the span of my hips, the stride of my step, the curve of my lips, because . . .' and I raised my hand.

'We are phenomenal women,' the crowd cried.

I replied, 'Phenomenal woman, that's me. I walk into a room just as cool as you please, and many try to cut me down to my knees, they can't touch my inner mystery. I say it's the fire in my eyes, the flash of my teeth, the swing of my waist, the joy in my feet, because . . .'

And the crowd said again, 'We are phenomenal women.'

And I replied, 'Phenomenal woman, that's me . . . Now you understand just why my head's not bowed. I don't shout or jump about or have to talk real loud, when you see me passing, it ought to make you proud. I say it's in the click of my heels, the kink of my hair, the palm of my hand, the need for my care, because we are phenomenal women. Phenomenal woman, that's me.'

I hoped that my own rewriting of Angelou's poem was inspirational for the women in that room, but the words also spoke to feelings I wished I could have expressed as chair of the Women's PLP. In any case, I recited my message loud and clear.

Shortly after the conference, I led the Phenomenal Woman Tour across the country. My mission was to empower women from all walks of life to stand for office, through training sessions, talks and meetings. It's been humbling to hear from many women, who have let me know that the tour gave them the confidence to stand as councillors and MPs in their local areas. Not only did the tour uplift them, it motivated and nourished me as well. I have always found that helping others grow fulfils me and adds to my own development. There have been times throughout my life when I have given a bit of myself and felt disappointed by others, times when I have gone the extra mile only to be betrayed. But there are times when

I have given a bit of myself and have seen my efforts blossom and come back in many ways, leaving me feeling that the work I do is ultimately worth it. Never stop doing good.

I met a lot of amazing people through my role as shadow secretary of state for women and equalities, engaging with all kinds of communities including LGBTQI+ groups. It's in my DNA to champion change, and as an MP with a platform and the power to push for progress, it's important for me to do so, not just within the Black community but for others that are just as marginalized. We all need to stand together. Being the lone voice can be tiring – it's too much responsibility being the only Black person in a workplace, for example, or the only gay person or the only disabled or working-class person, especially when surrounded by a majority of people who have the luxury of never experiencing the issues you may face. I know this means my presence really matters in Parliament, especially when we consider my upbringing and family, where I grew up, and the constituency I represent. I know that the information that comes out of my mouth might not be properly received by an audience who doesn't know how to relate to me. Once we get the conversations flowing, it's important to have allies who will help to spread our message. Hearing it from someone who looks like us or identifies as we do often helps a message land better. We need to have allies and we need to be allies.

I use my voice where I can, to ensure people aren't forgotten in debates and policies: fighting for someone else's equality doesn't erode my own. Often it seems the privileged believe that if they allow the oppressed to receive equal rights, they themselves get fewer, when all it really means is a more equal or equitable playing field for all. You don't have to be Black to advocate for a Black person. You don't have to be gay to advocate for a gay person. You don't have to be disabled to advocate for a disabled person. And generally I have found that it's easier to advocate for others than it is to advocate for yourself. If we can get to a place where more people are advocating for those who don't look or act like them we can move the dial a lot quicker.

In 2018, I won the *DIVA* Ally of the Year Award. The year after that, *PinkNews* wrote that I was 'one of the LGBT community's fiercest allies in Parliament'.[5] Both acknowledgements meant a lot to me. Being the best ally possible isn't just about politics or winning support, it's simply personal. In my late teens one of my closest friends, Alan, came out to me, and I was most surprised to learn that he feared telling me because he had already lost friends along the way. (In all honesty, I was annoyed because I wasn't the first friend he had told!) He didn't want to lose me too, he said, but all I had to say was 'Cool.' It didn't matter to me. All I wanted was for him to be his true, authentic self. It made me sad to realize he felt such shame around his sexuality that it needed to be kept secret. It also made me laugh because he was the only boy my mum ever allowed to come into my bedroom. He is still a very close friend, and many other friends have come out to me since. It's only natural that I lend my voice where and for whoever I can.

Equality is equality, and everyone deserves it. And just as I won't stand for racism and sexism, I won't stand for homophobia or transphobia either, the latter of which is becoming a distraction tool for today's government. 'Othering' is a tool used to dehumanize people so that those in power can discriminate against them and treat them more harshly. Just look back in history, at slavery and the creation of racial divides, the Holocaust and the othering of Jews, gay people and Section 28, now trans people and refugees.

Abstaining from hate and protecting those who are particularly vulnerable to physical and emotional attack is a no-brainer to me. During the *PinkNews* Awards in October 2019, I spoke out about the government's delays to reform the Gender Recognition Act (GRA) and condemned the way some politicians were slow to act because of anti-trans sentiments. The Act has the potential to allow trans people to live and die in the gender they associate with.

The government deliberately delayed on this reform, which has created a hostile environment for trans people. They claimed that allowing trans women into single-sex spaces would mean men were routinely allowed there too. The law actually states:

> If a service provider provides single- or separate-sex services for women and men, or provides services differently to women and men, they should treat

transsexual people according to the gender role in which they present. However, the Act does permit the service provider to provide a different service or exclude a person from the service who is proposing to undergo, is undergoing or who has undergone gender reassignment. This will only be lawful where the exclusion is a proportionate means of achieving a legitimate aim.[6]

So the Equality Act (2010) and the Gender Recognition Act (2004) have no bearing on each other, and the announcement also mentioned that there will be no change to trans people's protections under the Equality Act (2010). Trans people will continue to have access to single-sex spaces unless there is a proportionate and justifiable reason for them to be excluded. I urged Parliament in not-so-subtle language to sign the Bill, because if other countries, such as Argentina, Belgium, Colombia, Denmark, Ireland, India, Malta, Norway, Pakistan, Portugal and Uruguay, could reform their laws on gender recognition, why couldn't we? Scotland voted to pass a law in December 2022. But in an unprecedented move, the British government has made an order under Section 35 of the Scotland Act 1998 to block the Gender Recognition Reform (Scotland) Bill, which contains amendments to the Gender Recognition Act 2004, from receiving Royal Assent. The ongoing debate here has caused extreme distress and divisions within sections of the LGBTQI+ community, and Westminster's stubborn approach isn't helping.

The work I was able to do under Jeremy Corbyn and the connections that I was able to build were liberating. Prior to becoming shadow secretary of state for women and equalities, I was shadow minister for Black and minority ethnic communities for just under a year. Between the two positions, I was able to get off the ground initiatives I cared passionately about. I was given the authority to do whatever I felt was right as long as anything that involved spending money was cleared by the shadow Treasury team. When I brought forward the Emancipation Educational Trust, an initiative to decolonize school curricula and to promote a greater understanding of empire, colonialism, and imperial migration, Jeremy loved the idea and was excited by it, and had his own ideas to contribute.

The goal was to create a deeper and more truthful understanding of British history, which includes Black history, to help combat the false divisions that the far-right are working to create – an Us versus Them mentality. The curriculum sought to highlight the positive stories often hidden from our history lessons, while acknowledging the special wealth and beauty of Africa and the Caribbean. We had hoped that this could be something to implement if we won the next general election.

In general, it was wonderful to feel nurtured and supported, and to work with a leader who wasn't afraid of BAME issues and took an intersectional approach. We all need spaces where our ideas are respected and listened to, but I find this is often a privilege given to those who are seen inherently to have good ideas or whose ideas fit neatly into the demands of the status quo. In my opinion good management is about having a growth mindset in which you seek to expand your learning and that of those around you, and also to have an intersectional approach.

A leader with an intersectional approach won't be blind to their biases, so will be open to explore a broad variety of ideas. They won't shut down opportunities before they've even had a chance to get off the ground, and will do the work to examine whether systems and processes are working in the way they should, not just in the way they always have. If everyone in your inner circle looks and thinks like you there will be little diversity in your outcomes.

7

WHO'S THE LIAR NOW?

ON 7 NOVEMBER 2019, I took a huge leap of faith and announced on Bloomberg UK TV that I would stand in the race for Labour's new deputy leader. The day before, Jeremy Corbyn's deputy leader, Tom Watson, had resigned for personal reasons. In my mind, there was no better time for Labour finally to have female representation at the top of the party.

After a devastating loss in the general election, I was determined to play a pivotal role in campaigning for the party with the hope of forming the next Labour government, and what better way to do that than through the role of deputy leader? As shadow secretary of state for women and equalities, I wanted to build upon the work I was already doing. I was the only candidate to serve under two Labour prime ministers, as well as in Corbyn's shadow cabinet, so I thought I was in a strong position to unite the party and take us forward.

The next couple of months saw my opponents come forward, including Rosena Allin-Khan, Richard Burgon,

Ian Murray and Angela Rayner, who was slated to be the popular candidate. No matter. I would roll up my sleeves and work hard to do what I needed to do to win. To make the ballot paper, I needed to secure twenty-two nominations from fellow MPs and MEPs, and later, support from five per cent of constituency Labour parties (CLPs) or three affiliate organizations, including two trade unions.

I put together a manifesto for a strategy that I could implement and took inspiration from my trade-union days. To the CORE programme (Campaign, Organize, Recruit and Educate) I would later add a D for Discipline. My manifesto would serve to ensure that Labour did all it could to reach out locally to a wide array of communities, because the party needed to build trust in the people after the last general election.

The organizing component would help train coordinators to arrange campaigns in every area, not just in large cities but in smaller towns and rural areas from the south-west to Scotland. Recruitment would prioritize structuring our party with diverse thoughts and ideas, and education would create programmes designed by people with lived experience, with Labour values at the core.

My programme would include training on everything from antiSemitism, Afriphobia, racism against African-Caribbean people, transphobia, misogyny, homophobia and other kinds of bullying and oppression, together with mental health and disability-awareness training.

Discipline was to learn the lesson that people do not vote for a disunited party. At the heart of this, I wanted to introduce cutting-edge technologies and campaign techniques that could help us reach out to new people and demographics. There was something quite energizing about imagining the ways I could bring the party together as a united force, and what felt key to that was being able to draw upon everyone's talents.

The ideas were flowing, and I was excited to share them, but it wasn't long before I became aware that ideas could take me only so far. I hadn't put too much thought into the financial side of things. I didn't have a rule book to guide me or an adviser to educate me, and while some MPs have their eye on future positions from the beginning of their career and plan accordingly, my mistake was to believe that grit, determination, ideas and hard work would win me the campaign. I failed to realize how much money it required to get your message to the members. My team and I had managed to fundraise around £30,000 but I hadn't considered that others could access and spend hundreds of thousands of pounds to power their campaigns. And so, for the next couple of months, my team and I persevered through a series of challenges, some more entertaining than others.

After my announcement it was time to prepare a team and organize. First, we needed a campaign office. I had a small team and a group of volunteers, and we all found ourselves shuttling from one place to another because money was so tight. With the help of a good friend,

Husayn, we rented an office in a WeWork, a shared community working space, doing a couple of days a week, but it was becoming clear to me that we needed a firm base. I started asking around, despite how much I dislike asking for favours. But if you don't ask, you don't get, and an interesting lead came in from a friend of a friend who had space above a Londis convenience shop. I asked my friend Guna how we were to access it, and he replied: 'You go into the Londis, and then you go to the milk cabinet. Behind that there's a secret door. You go up the stairs . . .' And, honestly, it all sounded a bit mad, but my team and I went to check it out anyway.

The space was literally as he had described it. I recorded myself walking past the milk cabinet, going up the secret flight of stairs, and entering this massive space that my team later dubbed 'The West and East Wing'.

I will never forget travelling around the country to launch our grassroots campaign. My campaign manager Carmel scrimped and scraped on train tickets and budget hotels, one of which turned out to be a complete nightmare. In one city, she booked my team of four (comprising of me, Carmel, Daniel and Carleen) into what basically looked like a brothel. Never have I seen so many boxes of tissues in my life, every time we turned there was yet another to haunt us.

Out of curiosity, I googled the place to find out what on earth we'd landed on and found out it had been voted the worst hotel in the country eight years running. I could see why. The door handle to our room had been kicked in so many times you could see where the lock had moved. The floors looked like they hadn't been cleaned in years (I was scared to put my feet on the carpet), and I couldn't find how to flush the toilet. The water didn't work. The shower didn't work. It was bloody awful. And we were skint, so we had to share a room. I couldn't sleep that night, and sat upright in my bed with my feet hanging over the side so they didn't touch the floor, cussing Carmel in my head and wondering how we'd got into this mess. Carmel, who also couldn't sleep, turned in her small bed and saw me glaring at her. We burst out laughing. But we weren't on holiday: we had a job to do, so we just had to stomach it and keep track of the bigger picture.

It was the members' events and hustings that more than made up for the mishaps. We brought real energy to the campaign and strove to engage people who were often overlooked. My motivational pitch came from a song that I'm infamous for quoting, but what can I say about Labi Siffre's 'Something Inside So Strong'? It's a song that's part of my heart – his words, which I've committed to memory, act like a lifeline or a rallying cry. They give me strength in times of need. In my youth, before it was possible to pull up the lyrics of a song on Google, I taped and listened to a song, then painstakingly wrote down the lyrics to commit them to heart. I'd listen to the song repeatedly to make sure I'd got the words down right, all while singing along to the tune. Listening, writing, replaying leave an imprint in your mind – the words become a part of you.

As you know, music informs and strengthens my values, so when I share these lyrics with the public, it's like leaving a part of me with them. It's also a way to unite the audience and liven up an event. For example, at the Women's Labour Party Conference of 2019, in reference to my policy aiming to implement flexible working, I quoted the great 'philosopher' Dolly Parton's lament about working from nine to five. I'm not ashamed of using lyrics in my speeches, but during the campaign – and almost as if on cue – a right-wing commentator tried to embarrass me by clipping together all the times I cited lyrics on the campaign trail. He put the mash-up on Twitter as an attack piece, but I thanked him. I wouldn't have had the time to compile the clips myself.

My team and I travelled all over Great Britain. I had different people volunteering at different times. I became friends with Linda Riley, the publisher of *DIVA* magazine, and she was a godsend. She took time out of her busy schedule and drove us around. In Cardiff, Wales, we came across voters who told us that no one from the party had ever visited them before. It was an eye-opening experience, going to a lot of red-wall seats across the Midlands and northern England, which I found to be warm and welcoming. In Birmingham, I made a speech at a members' event, and the highlight of the afternoon was when a young man approached me afterwards to say, 'Dawn, thank you for saving my life ... and meet my daughter.' At first, I couldn't be sure who he was, but as he introduced himself, it dawned on me that he had come to my offices in Brent and Westminster for an internship many years ago.

At a time when it was easier for the public to access passes to come to Parliament, I offered work experience to young people aged between fourteen and sixteen. I wanted the youth of Brent to have access to an institution they might not have felt they belonged to. Just as their more privileged peers had access to prestigious connections, it was fundamental that I extended the same opportunity to the kids of my constituency, who were typically barred from such advantages. So, if those kids could put on their CVs and college applications that they had worked for an MP it would count for something. But there was no proper system to reimburse interns. Parliament gives MPs one pot of money to pay their staff. So, if I wanted to offer this opportunity, I had to fund it myself. I put any money I made from TV appearances into a pot to pay for their food and travel so that my interns wouldn't be out of pocket. The Labour Party now has a policy of no unpaid interns which I fully support.

The young man standing in front of me had been heading down a very destructive path when he came to my offices. On top of that, a friend of his had been murdered, and he was spiralling into depression. He ended up shadowing me and working with my team assiduously. After the experience, his mum thanked me for what I'd done for his mental health and sense of wellbeing. But it was the least I could do. I only hoped the experience would do him some good. And now here he was, at a Labour Party members' event after all these years, married and with a young child. I cried.

*

I was in Leicester, listening to party members in a community hall, when I saw there was no chance I'd win the deputy leadership race. Members were complaining about receiving a text from every other candidate in the race apart from me. My core team sat me down and explained that we didn't have the money to send texts to Labour members. At just 2p per text it would cost at least £15,000 to send just one text to members, and candidates needed to send at least two. Tens of thousands of pounds, money we simply did not have. My heart sank. I had been second in the polling until then and, just like that, I had been priced out of the race. Why did it cost so much? Why were candidates excluded from using the already established party systems to communicate with members?

Texts were not the only thing I couldn't afford: I couldn't write to every eligible voter as this could cost as much as £454,000. Also, if I made it to the ballot, there would be a £2,500 charge for the membership list and £2,500 for the affiliates list. Shockingly, that's £5,000 for access to the party's Excel spreadsheet. We also couldn't afford an app, rumoured to come to £13,000, so we organized traditional small, localized phone sessions. How could the Labour Party justify these costs? It was enough to put off any working-class or disadvantaged candidate from running in future.

I strongly believe there is no reason why candidates should spend, in some cases, over a million pounds to get elected in internal elections. When looking at reforming politics and including the excluded, we need to consider what stops people participating in the first place. Some just do not have the funds or the connections to access thousands of pounds to become a candidate. If we really want to reach out to 'ordinary' people, we have to remove this financial burden. Making the system fairer and less expensive would ensure that we have a broader selection of candidates. If we only elect people who have lots of money or access to lots of money, what does that say about us as a political party? At this critical time, we should be investing in ideas and a vision to change society.

When the hard truth of the situation hit me, I wondered at what point we should give up. I didn't want to let people down, neither my team nor the people who supported me, nor the thousands who had already voted for me. I surveyed the room, saw the faces of the two people working closest with me, including my new best mate Linda Riley, who had become like a campaign manager, and my volunteers, and said, 'Look, even though we're not going to win this, we've built something powerful. We've given people hope. We've engaged people who haven't been engaged before. Let's leave this race with our heads held high. Let's still campaign to win and let's just have the most fun that we can possibly have to the very end.' And we maintained that attitude until the last day.

*

In the year of the deputy-leadership race, the Covid-19 pandemic of 2020 would change the world for ever, creating national pain and loss, alongside cronyism and corruption within the Tory Party. Over the next couple of years, the country would go into lockdown on numerous occasions, widespread panic would leave shelves empty in supermarkets, Covid cases would rise, resulting in hundreds of thousands of deaths, and the NHS would be overrun with little support from the government apart from public hand-clapping. Most of the public, except for key workers, would work from home, with much of the nation on furlough. People lost loved ones, including myself, while many struggled through the aftermath of the illness, and others gained a new outlook on life. The next couple of years would be catastrophic emotionally, economically and politically, as the individuals making the rules were meanwhile breaking them behind closed doors, travelling during lockdown, having parties and gatherings, and ensuring that, through a VIP fast-track system, Tory donors were lining their pockets with millions of taxpayers' pounds.

While it was unpopular to do so, as I mentioned earlier, I questioned the former health secretary, Matt Hancock, during Science and Technology Committee meetings. I made it clear that I wouldn't back down from enquiries into PPE deals becoming public knowledge. The government had used the pandemic as a smokescreen to do all the things they always dreamed of implementing but never had the power or permission to do. Not only were they finding opportunities to profit from PPE, but they were looking to make money from gathering and selling the nation's personal data. The Conservatives were attempting to strike a troubling deal with the American software company Palantir, co-founded by Peter Thiel, an entrepreneur who had backed Donald Trump's presidential campaign. Palantir offered to move NHS data to a centralized database for a worrying £1, only to win a contract later for £23.5 million.

In June 2021, I questioned Hancock's claim that people were enthusiastic about giving up sensitive patient data without consent and asked him about the contract with Palantir. I highlighted the fact that Amnesty International and other organizations had raised concerns about the safety and privacy of our data and medical histories in one database, especially if that data was sold to other people or weaponized against us.

As a member of the Science and Technology Committee I had been closely examining the government's PPE procurement, and had written letters to the then prime minister, Boris Johnson, as far back as 2020 questioning one of many things: that contracts appeared to be given to unknown firms with meagre capital, few or no staff, little trading history, and no prior experience in delivering or dealing with PPE. Many of these firms appeared to be offshore. *Byline Times* reported that several contracts awarded were to companies owned or run by prominent Conservative Party supporters – billions of pounds in fact were paid to firms with links to the Tory Party.[1] PPE, such as gowns and masks, supplied by various companies, was found to be defective and it was unclear at the time whether a refund for these items was solicited.

The lack of due diligence was apparent with many news sources calling attention to the scandal unfolding in front of our eyes. For the next three years, I used every opportunity to try to get to the bottom of what was truly going on behind the scenes, working with the investigative journalists who broke many of the stories at *Byline Times*, and the Good Law Project, a not-for-profit organization relentlessly pursuing the truth, even in court, about the government's procurement contracts. But with every question I posed, the answers were sparse, requiring a diligent piecing together of insufficient information.

One event after another seemed to occur in quick succession during the summer of 2020, so much so it was difficult to keep up. It's true that the modern world hadn't suffered a pandemic of this scale for some time, but the inability of our government to grasp the reins was becoming obvious, especially in comparison to other countries. Boris Johnson's cabinet was unravelling behind the scenes, and unclear and confusing pandemic rules were issued almost daily. Restrictions were eased, establishments allowed to open their doors, the public advised to keep a metre apart, and we were all encouraged to eat out to help out.

In the United States, the death of George Floyd in Minnesota at the hands of the police sparked worldwide shock and outrage. Our lives indoors behind our screens intensified a conscious reckoning around deep-rooted systemic issues that had not previously been contended with on such a national and international level. Black Lives Matter protests in the UK prompted difficult discussions around race (and supposed national safety) across the media and between friends and families. Companies were making sometimes empty pledges to prioritize and re-examine their diversity and inclusion policies, and individuals were actively thinking about their own biases.

Here was a chance for people of colour to be listened to and heard online, in the media or through literature as they spoke about their lived experiences of racism and unconscious bias. I was invited to speak about these issues on several platforms, but the death of George Floyd and the 'disruption' of the Black Lives Matter protests weren't the only pressing issues: it was now known that Covid was disproportionately affecting and killing people of colour.

Immediately after I spoke about these issues publicly, the racist abuse from keyboard warriors poured in. Abusive messages were left on the constituency-office answer machine, the Willesden office frontage was smashed, and then an object, something like a brick, was thrown through the window after office hours. I was already acutely attuned to my staff's and my safety: we were no strangers to such intense attacks.

During the general election period in 2017, a man burst into our reception area with a golf club. His attempt to break through the door into the room where I saw constituents was thwarted by a few members of staff, who pushed him out of the building and slammed the door before he could attack me. Instinctively a member of staff and my campaign agent, Tom, ran after him to get a photo. The man dropped his golf club and took off. I couldn't have lived with myself if someone had attacked anyone trying to defend me. It's frightening to think of what might have happened that day if the man with the golf club had brought a gun or a knife. Reality kicked in when one of my staff showed up to work that week with a stab-proof vest and gloves to wear to surgeries.

The threat of violence felt even worse in 2020, and the continued abuse, threats and incidents were affecting my staff and making our working environment unsafe. The rise in rent and the inability to socially distance also played a role in my decision to close our constituency office. As an MP, it's important for me to be accessible to my constituents, and for them to see me in person, but I also have to make assessments around safety. I now hold surgeries only in public places that have security, or I will inform the police so that they can provide non-invasive support.

Sadly, this didn't start with the events of that summer, but with the string of plots and fatal attacks against other MPs. My friend Jo Cox was murdered by a right-wing extremist in 2016. Two years later, a plot by a neo-Nazi to kill another friend, Rosie Cooper, was thwarted, and three years after that David Amess was also murdered in an act of terrorism. MPs have been forced to take measures into their own hands when it comes to keeping themselves safe, which isn't always easy when you're out and about all the time, engaging in public events. When people approach me in public, it's hard to tell sometimes whether their intentions are good or bad, especially if someone isn't smiling.

I'm vigilant at the best of times, but towards the end of 2018, on the Jubilee Line, I was caught off guard during rush-hour while listening to music (through one earphone, for safety reasons) in a packed carriage. A woman came through one of the interconnecting doors, stuck her face into mine, and said aggressively, 'Dawn Butler, let's talk about this.' She proceeded to swear at me, calling me a 'fucking bitch' and a 'fucking slag' then demanded to know why I hadn't helped her daughters. I hadn't been able to place her until she said that, and it clicked: we'd spoken during one of my surgeries in Willesden. I was shocked to see her on the train with me, nowhere near the constituency office.

'What are you doing here?' I asked, starting to feel a bit nervous.

'I followed you, bitch,' she said, matter of fact, and

later an eyewitness reported her saying, 'I always know where you are. I always know your schedule.'

She asked me if we were going to talk about the situation or if she was 'going to have to kill somebody'.

I asked, 'Do you think that's a wise thing to say?'

'I don't care. I will kill you.'

At that point I wasn't sure what she was going to do, but I knew it was time to escape because her behaviour was erratic, and it was unclear to me whether she was carrying a weapon. I stood up slowly with my rucksack in front of me in case she had a knife. The other people on the train must have been communicating to each other: when we got to Willesden, someone pushed her out of the door and called the police. I sat down, shaking, pretending I was okay, but the guy next to me noticed and said, 'I think you're in shock.' The passengers around me also apologized for letting it go on for so long – at first they'd thought we were friends and just talking. (I was very grateful for the kindness of strangers that day, and never could have imagined I'd meet any of them again. But when I fell ill with a serious infection, the man who had sat next to me on that tube came into my life once more, when he accompanied me in the ambulance to hospital as the paramedic. When he reminded me of who he was, I was stunned, and said, 'You must be my guardian angel.')

Now I make sure that the police are aware of my every activity, and I carry a personal tracker alarm with me everywhere I go, as well as taking other necessary measures. As a public figure vulnerable to attack, whether in person or online, I've learned to be more careful, cautious, and to take everything seriously. That includes every threat or nasty message that comes my way online. People have never been shy about sharing what they think of me. The majority of the time it's positive, but it can often be vile and rude, and just plain surprising to think that people hate you so much they go out of their way to threaten your life.

Such irrational behaviour isn't upsetting just for me, it's upsetting for my staff, who come across, read, and field these messages daily. We have a folder for certain parliamentary emails labelled 'Abuse', and if the content of any reaches a certain threshold, we send them to the police to investigate. The police haven't always been minded to pursue these cases, but they've got better over the years, especially with a change of management, and they are now taking them more seriously. Individuals who have sent threatening or abusive messages in the past have been jailed or given suspended sentences of up to twelve weeks. In other cases, people have been found guilty of sending an offensive email to a parliamentary address. It's reassuring to know that measures are in place to tackle the abuse, and that the police and the courts are now sending a clear message to people who feel entitled to send abusive communications.

Holding people to account on Twitter is much more difficult – and was even before Elon Musk took over the platform. I tend not to scroll, so I don't see everything that's directed at me, but if a member of my team catches a concerning message, they'll report it, despite the threshold for action being higher. In the past, we've got into arguments with the company around what they deem actionable, questioning whether someone threatening to hang me isn't a cause for concern.

In February 2021, Tan Dhesi, MP, alerted me to a very disturbing tweet directed at me by a man named Stephen Peddie, who happened to stand for the Brexit Party in 2019: 'Egregious theft in time of national emergency. Someone please explain to me why a bullet to the back of the head is anything but justified and wholly deserved.'[2] Unknown to me, Peddie had written this in response to a false story about me that Toby Young had reshared on Twitter. Shortly after the tweet was reported, the police called to say they'd been to his house in Kent and had confiscated a legally owned firearm. That he owned a gun made me freeze, and I was at a loss for words. It was hard to keep my emotions in check, knowing that his words might have constituted a genuine death threat. In court, he claimed, 'I could not have reasonably expected Dawn Butler to have seen my tweet on Young's account and she didn't. She was sent the tweet by a third party.'

It was shocking to hear such an excuse – even if I hadn't seen the tweet, what he had said, and on a public forum no less, was dangerous, troubling and upsetting, especially in response to someone with a large number of followers.

I cannot ignore the abuse I face online or become desensitized to it, because it will encourage others to continue the same behaviour. His defence rang alarm bells for me and made me wonder what else people were getting up to online that we didn't see. And what were they doing offline? We know that extreme groups spread hate and falsehoods; we also know that Incels (a subculture of hostile men who regard themselves as involuntarily celibate and unable to find a romantic partner) are a very dangerous group. It is a growing problem, and the threats are serious and credible. Peddie was convicted in the end and given a suspended sentence. I thought this was insufficient, but I hope he is never again able to own a firearm and will be banned from standing for public office.

Our brains are programmed to identify danger so that we can protect ourselves, but that means negative comments tend to stick in the mind. To counter the heavy load of the 'Abuse' folder, we also keep a folder full of positive messages, and I am delighted to say that I have more nice ones than negative ones. It's important to focus on the good stuff. We should do whatever we can to train our brains to hold on to the light.

*

Around the same time, a pressure pot of tensions and emotions began bubbling up across the entire country. The damage the Tory government was doing to the nation in a time of great suffering was disheartening and it appeared that no one was doing anything about it. Our democracy was on the line and seemed to be slipping into the grip of fascistic governance by the day. There were so many fires to put out politically that it was becoming difficult for people to focus and concentrate on a single issue, and this felt deliberate: keep the people confused so that we all walk blindly into an authoritarian state.

What particularly angered me was the long list of Boris Johnson's lies in the House of Commons. He lied about the economy growing by about 73 per cent. He lied about reinstating nurses' bursaries. He lied about the Tories investing £34 billion in the NHS. He lied about the government severing the link between infection, serious disease and death. I wrote a letter to the prime minister in September 2020, enquiring about PPE, and signed early-day motions (short proposals that give MPs a chance to express an opinion and raise a particular cause for support) demanding the truth, but answers weren't forthcoming. I approached the leader of the Labour Party, Keir Starmer, who I had served with in the shadow cabinet, who by this point had taken over from Jeremy Corbyn, to ask if we could hold a debate on the prime minister's lies. He said he would approach the whips but, months later, nothing happened, and all I heard was the familiar refrain, 'There's nothing that can be done.' Keir was restricted by outdated Parliamentary procedures. I look forward to a Labour government where experienced and knowledgeable MPs like me are utilized to modernize parliament and to reform our constitution so we can deal with the current economic and social challenges faced in every area of our country.

Deep down, I knew I couldn't accept no for an answer. If the system was failing us, we needed to do something to radically reform it. The common theme of the reports coming out about the government centred on a kind of arrogance and corruption all rooted in privilege and entitlement. These people could play the system and get away with it because they had always been allowed to do so. They often played the system without remorse or without thinking about how it affected the public or other individuals.

The tipping point for me came during the Charlie Elphicke sexual-assault case, when it was revealed that five Tory MPs had attempted to influence judges on the overall decision. Here was a man who was later found guilty of three counts of sexual assault while serving as an MP, yet his friends and colleagues were trying to sway the judges to lessen any forthcoming penalties. The MPs were suspended from the Commons for a single day – a single day – despite blatantly damaging public trust in the rule of law.

There's a reason why the judicial system remains independent and impartial, yet Tory MPs tried to manipulate the system and, worse, were hardly reprimanded for doing so. It was at this point that I decided enough was enough, and it was time to call out Boris Johnson on his lies. In many ways, it wasn't just about the prime minister – someone who was supposed to be leading by example – but also about the other representatives of the party who were continuously undermining our democracy by blatantly exhibiting unacceptable behaviour without any account-ability whatsoever.

On 22 July 2021, I stood on the floor of the House and made a speech critiquing the prime minister's behaviour to date, and I very purposely called him a liar. A few people were present in the chamber that day, and we were all trying to socially distance while wearing masks. I read out a few of the lies Johnson had told, as reported by Peter Stefanovic from the Communication Workers Union (CWU) who had done amazing work researching and fact-checking Johnson's mistruths. I finished my speech by declaring that the prime minister had lied to the House and to the country over and over again, and when I said that, there were murmurs of strong disap-proval in the House.

The deputy speaker called, 'Order, order,' and added, 'I'm sure that the member will reflect on her words just then and perhaps correct the record,' but I refused. Instead of retracting, I repeated what I had said, that the prime minister had lied to this House time and time again. 'And it's funny,' I said, 'that we get in trouble in this place for calling out the lie rather than the person lying.' The deputy speaker again called, 'Order,' and asked me to withdraw my words, but someone needed to tell the truth in the House, so I refused once again. The deputy speaker had no choice but to throw me out as per parliamentary protocol. On some level, I knew there would be consequences that day, and I was prepared to face them — to a certain extent. I was asked to leave the chamber, but I didn't think I'd have to leave the parliamentary estate immediately! I was grateful I had my house keys on me.

After five minutes, my phone was ringing non-stop and I realized that I didn't want to go home in case the press were waiting for me outside my house. I was a little rattled, so I called my wonderful friend Linda Riley and said, 'I need to hide somewhere – I'm coming to your house.' She asked me what I was talking about and I told her the press were after me. Linda thought I was exaggerating until she turned on *Sky News* and saw me as the leading story.

I didn't know what I'd expected to happen – I hadn't thought that far – but I knew in my gut that I'd done what I felt was right. I'd had to call it out and draw attention to his lies, as it seemed he was getting away with it. I never would have been happy with myself knowing I was part of a broken system that was allowing a liar to ride roughshod over our democracy. As an MP, I couldn't allow myself to turn a blind eye, and felt it was my duty to speak truth to power. So, I broke the rule, an outdated, archaic rule that says a parliamentarian cannot call another parliamentarian a liar. However, the irony is that the prime minister was allowed to stand at the despatch box and lie to the country and Parliament repeatedly without consequence.

In that instance, I believed the rule needed to be broken, not just for the greater good but also for a sense of justice. The nation didn't deserve this, especially not during a worldwide pandemic. We couldn't keep allowing the government to create rules they required everyone else to follow while they made separate rules for themselves.

When I called Boris Johnson a liar that day, I hadn't expected my own party to make me feel temporarily disowned, but they went completely silent after the incident and surprisingly gave me the cold shoulder. At a certain point, I even received messages asking if I'd done it to embarrass the deputy speaker. *What?* I clearly spoke to call out Boris Johnson's lies: why couldn't my party see that? I could almost sense Labour going around behind closed doors saying, 'Shit! What has she done now?' A few members of the party were even interviewed on television shortly after but refused to mention me by name as if I were a public disgrace that they wanted no association with. I noticed that a few Labour MPs were no longer following me on social media.

The aftermath of my actions was uncomfortable for a short while, and in that time, what struck me most was the lengths to which people would go to find a reason as to why I had done what I did other than the most obvious. It became clear to me that the parliamentary system, no matter which side of the fence you were on, was complicit in Boris Johnson's lies, and it was not robust enough to stop the man or his government doing harm. Instead, I was being punished for attempting to bring to light an unjust situation. One phone call in particular from Anthony Watson stood out to me. He told me to be strong and resolute and to believe in what I am standing for. 'You change the system,' he said. Anthony is a gay man who went from being a homeless man to founding The Bank of London. His advice to me is always so powerful.

For some people, Boris Johnson lying was not a big deal because of his track record – he'd been sacked from previous posts for the same type of behaviour. But now he was in a great position of power and his lies, at this extraordinary time in history, had real consequences. To give one example, he'd explicitly stated in Parliament that 'all guidance was followed completely in No 10', when he was questioned about a Downing Street Christmas party. But as we now know, multiple gatherings took place which broke the very rules that the government set out, with Boris himself receiving a Fixed Penalty Notice. Others, even if they agreed with the sentiment of what I'd said, were terrified of appearing 'unparliamentary' and thought I shouldn't be so direct in calling it out.

It was disappointing to discover that many people were more concerned with their own reputations than with the issue of Boris Johnson's, but this is common behaviour many of us will routinely have experienced throughout our lives. Despite the obvious truth, no one would step in to support me until they could ensure that what I had done was the popular thing to do – not the right thing but the popular thing. Their initial hesitancy to have my back, in my mind, tied into the ways I have always been perceived and treated within the institution where unconscious bias clouds better judgement and obscures clarity. If I had been a white man or a white woman, who was totally supported no matter what, my words might have been received differently – there would have been no question around intention. But because I'm a Black woman who is known to be outspoken – and not in a 'breath of fresh air' kind of way – within the establishment, I believe my message was lost, and the focus was on how my words were too strong.

When people are punished for calling out bad behaviour, it reveals the propensity of the system to ignore wrongdoing for the sake of a crippling decorum or, in the case of the police, to force loyalty. To me, it's one of the worst forms of gaslighting. It reminds me of when I had gone on BBC *Politics Live* earlier that year and made a comment about Boris Johnson being a racist because of numerous remarks he'd made throughout his career. It's well reported that he'd commented about Muslim women (calling them 'letterboxes') and African people (referring to them as 'piccaninnies' and describing them as having 'watermelon smiles'). Laura Trott, Conservative MP for Sevenoaks, took offence at my choice of words (instead of Johnson's), admonishing me for being 'rude' and 'offensive'. It was 'outrageous' that I would call him a racist, and by doing so, I was 'undermining politics and political discourse'.[3] And yet his opinions and choice of words was not deemed unprofessional or inexcusable or hurtful or bigoted, just 'robust and unfortunate' as one broadcaster said. Instead, I was the one behaving poorly.

A video of my 'Boris is a liar' speech was posted online

and viewed millions of times within twenty-four hours, and this solidarity from the public helped massively. If the public hadn't been behind me, I am sure someone would have asked me to apologize for breaking parliamentary protocol. I received at least three thousand emails containing supportive messages for what I had done, a groundswell of support from outside Parliament. I refrained from doing the rounds on television, despite media requests, and chose to do one interview for the independent news source *Byline TV*. I also did one radio show with James O'Brien, and one podcast with Owen Jones. It was for everybody else to debate whether calling out the lie was worse than the lies themselves, and that was exactly what began to happen.

All I ever wanted was for the lies to stop, and I hoped that taking the first courageous step would be the start of a serious conversation about how unsuitable Boris Johnson was for the role of prime minister. It was nerve-racking to stand on the floor and stick to my guns, but in the end, it was worth it. If I hadn't been kicked out of Parliament, and if social media hadn't existed, the point I made wouldn't have been taken seriously.

There's never a simple route when you're challenging the status quo because the pushback is phenomenal. Despite this, I felt a responsibility to speak the truth and for people to know the truth. We shouldn't fear questioning and challenging the systems that are meant to protect and advocate for us, because we live in a democracy and it should be our right to do so. Change can happen only when we're willing to ask the hard questions, when we're willing to point out what we feel is unjust and wrong.

The people the system works for will have no interest in change because it serves them well. These people aren't going to turn around and say, 'Oh dear, yes, I can understand that's not working,' because they're benefiting and profiting from a system that's been designed for them. In many ways, because our systems were never designed for someone like me, I have always found myself to be a lone wolf able to see the ways it disadvantages a multitude of others.

Some may say I am a disruptor, and sometimes, to agitate for change, it's important to sacrifice your comfort, but I understand that not everyone has the capacity to do this. But if you have the courage, time and mental capacity to step out on your own and speak those uncomfortable truths, then the price is worth it, because you're not just doing it for yourself, but for everybody else as well. You might feel alone in taking those initial steps, you might feel lonely, but along the way there will be others who see the strength in your determination and fight.

I want people to understand that they have personal power, unique to them. And if you feel otherwise, you've already given away your power. You either build on it, exercise it, or you restrict and diminish it. And if so, what are you going to do? What road are you going to take? We've all got platforms and ways of exerting our voice and power. Politically, it could mean joining a party, becoming a local councillor or helping an MP. It could even be through voting or persuading a member of your family to vote. I know there are people out there who aren't that bothered about voting, but if you don't vote, then someone else takes your voice.

Apathy is what most gatekeepers, from executive boards to judging panels, rely on, and the injustices will continue as long as you disengage. Our systems will tie you up in knots, gaslight you, wrap you in red tape so that you don't complain or, worse, stay silent. But who does that serve other than those out for their own interests, or liars, or criminals dressed as government officials, or rapists, as in the case of a few bad police officers? Anyone can be involved in politics in a big or small way, and at this critical time, our democracy and our rights are on the line, so we should insist that we partake. We do not live in an authoritarian state, and we should not just let the rich and powerful make all the decisions while everyone else just sucks it up. Otherwise, we're in big trouble.

8

THE BODY NEEDS REST

A LOT CAN BE SAID ABOUT the physical and mental toll politics and activism may take, and by the end of 2021 I was exhausted beyond belief. How any of us survived the grief and stress of Covid and the political chaos that followed (and continues) is unbelievable. As you know, much of my energy comes from putting my all into fighting for others and giving voice to the powerless, and I hope I can do that for many years to come. But I was about to learn a new and even bigger lesson, one unconnected to politics, and all to do with my health. In many ways, I was still operating as the fearless girl of my youth, and the no-holds-barred woman I had become, picking and choosing my battles. Now I was confronted with a different sort of challenge, one I could not run from.

It was October 2021 when I received a mammogram appointment letter that I initially put to one side. It seemed too early and I didn't know when I was going to find the time to attend. I knew it was important but the last thing I wanted was to have my breasts squashed between plates while I moved around in awkward positions. I was familiar with the routine – my mum and sister had had breast cancer, and my male cousin Johnny had unfortunately died from it, and although I had tested negative for any of the breast cancer genes, I still needed to be examined regularly. I never looked forward to the appointments. I checked my breasts often, never noticing any warning signs like lumps around the breasts or underarms, or inverted/leaking nipples, or redness/flaking in the same areas, so I wasn't worried, but I knew it was important to go.

A couple of weeks after my routine appointment, I received a phone call from a withheld number while I was waiting outside a local school – I was their VIP guest. Attending school assemblies is good fun. I find young people engaging because they keep me on my toes with all their questions. Primary-school kids tend to ask how much I get paid, my age (I tell them I'm over forty, and they think I'm old), my favourite foods, and whether I've met any famous people (my answers Emeli Sandé, Kelly Holmes and Sinitta never impress them, mostly because they don't know who those people are). Sometimes they ask questions that make me stop and think, such as what three wishes I would want granted, or which superpower I would like to have. In response to the latter question, I have told kids that I'd like the power to persuade people to do what I think is right, to be able to pass positive laws and make society a better place. 'So, mind-bending!' they cried. And I thought, *Yeah, that would be great!*

Although the primary-school kids are charming, the junior-school kids are less innocent. I'm often surprised by what comes out of their mouths – that's when I think, *Oh, God, I'm really getting old.*

Before my school assembly, I had time on my hands, so I answered the call, thinking it was a journalist. As soon as I heard the woman at the other end, any possibility of a stress-free afternoon was ruined. I immediately recognized her voice from the breast-cancer reception desk, and after confirming I was Dawn Butler, she told me I needed to come in next Friday for a biopsy.

'A biopsy? Why do I need a biopsy? If I need a biopsy, that must mean you've found something. Have you found something?'

She stuttered, before checking that no one else had been in contact yet. I said that this was the first I was hearing about my mammogram results and that I was in complete shock. The words 'Is it my left breast?' left my mouth before I'd had a chance to think about them. I don't know why, but I suddenly remembered my left breast being particularly painful during the mammogram. She stumbled, then confirmed it was. She said, 'What we need to do . . . we can't do it that day. We'll need you in on Tuesday instead.'

At that moment I thought, *So, it's really bad. It isn't just a routine biopsy. They need additional expertise.* But I didn't have time to process any of this as I had to go into the school. I composed myself before watching a lovely assembly – the children were wonderful. Afterwards, one of the teachers said a little girl wanted to come and speak to me. I thought it was going to be a normal 'Thank you so much, Miss, for coming to our school and watching our assembly,' but it wasn't. Instead, the cutest little girl stood in front of me and said: 'Dawn Butler, thank you very much for rescuing me from Afghanistan.' I burst into tears, in front of all those kids. It was just an overload of emotion.

Shortly after the assembly, unsure of how to process the news I'd heard and trying to cope emotionally, I took out my phone and began recording the first of many video diaries. I believe in the power of expressing your thoughts and feelings, whether through writing or speaking, instead of bottling them up because at some stage those emotions will manifest in unproductive ways. It's a bit like running water: even if you try to stop the flow, it always finds a way to escape. The videos were just a few minutes long, but they helped me during a very painful time.

Video diary: So, I'm obviously not expecting to share these videos otherwise I'd put some bloody make-up on. I look rough. Anyway, this morning, Monday morning, my car battery's flat so I need to call the AA . . . It's a bit crazy today with this new Covid variant . . . and I'm feeling really emotional and teary, I think probably because I've got to go and see other people today. I don't really want to see anyone or talk to anyone; I just kind of want to know what's happening, what I'm doing, what's happening with my body . . . That's how I'm feeling today. So, every

day – I've got bags under my eyes – every day I will leave
my video diary even if it's just for a minute to say how I
feel and that's it. All right, it's Monday.

On the Tuesday, I had my biopsy. The experience was
nerve-racking, but the nurses were lovely and made me
feel at ease. There were three of them, and they were all
trying to find the right spot on my breast before extract-
ing the necessary fluid. The size of the long needle had
me looking away as directed, and I kept very still. All I
could hear was a vacuuming sound as they sucked out
the cells to be sent off to the lab.

I spent the next ten days desperately trying to distract
myself, but it was bloody difficult, especially because the
spot where they took the fluid was still quite painful. My
thoughts flipped between *Shit, I have cancer*, and then
Don't think like that, be positive! I still didn't want to tell
anyone except my other half, Mark, and my sister-in-law,
Tracy, because I didn't want them to worry and stress
themselves out. Basically, it was ten days of hell and the
odd glass of wine.

Video diary: This is what it's like after you've had a biopsy,
big needle in, lots of stuff out, keep it dry for six days . . . At
least it's done, results in ten days.

Video diary: . . . It's quite painful still, I have to take
paracetamol, not ibuprofen because that thins the blood . . .
Just hoping in ten days' time it comes back that it's okay,

but we'll have to wait . . . Try not to think about it for ten
days . . . I'm not quite sure I'm going to leave a diary every
day because that just reminds me, whereas I'm going to try
and forget because it'll be 23 December so let's see . . .

The two days before receiving my results I spent sobbing, feeling stressed and sad. I threw myself into work for my mental health and made plans to visit two schools. The kids would cheer me up. The schools were close to Mum, so I stayed at hers because of my early starts, but I still hadn't broken the news, so it was awkward. Christmas was only days away and I didn't want to ruin it for her or anyone else. But in the end I had to tell her, as she could tell I was sad. And, as I'd expected, she didn't take the news very well. That only confirmed I'd been right to keep the news close to my chest – it was too much having to take on and manage other people's reactions and emotions. Mine were enough.

I remember when Mum had cancer, she didn't talk about it very much and suffered in silence, as many Jamaican parents do. My parents never revealed personal information to their children, let alone their feelings. When I was younger, I took my parents to the hospital for the first time only to realize I didn't know when they were born. Because of this cultural trait, it felt easier to tell friends than to tell family. I ended up telling my staff about the cancer in the new year, and found the best way to break the news was to say, 'I've got some bad news but I'm not dying,' and that helped, but it was still bloody difficult.

The day before my results were due, I didn't want to burden friends and family with the anxiety of my waiting, but I wanted to speak to someone objective, so I plucked up the courage to call Parliament's Employee Assistance Programme, a confidential hotline for staff and their families available 24/7. I soon regretted my decision. I wanted to hear some reassuring words, but I was met with a load of questions: my name, date of birth, address, etc. My paranoia got the best of me. As an MP, I'm cautious about random people knowing intimate details about my life, in case they sell it to the papers. Even though this was seen as a confidential space, I was still sceptical about opening up as Dawn Butler, so I gave the guy the name and age of Carmel, my staff member. When he asked where I lived, I wanted to know why that was important. In a roundabout way, he said just in case I was feeling suicidal, they could send someone to the property.

It was all routine procedure, but the ten-minute-long checklist only served to exasperate me, so I gave up, and called the Samaritans instead. After another lengthy wait (I obviously don't do waiting well) I thought, *You know what? I'm not suicidal. I just want someone to talk to. There might be someone else who needs this service more.* So, I hung up, switched on the TV, and numbed myself with a load of crap instead. But since then, I have spoken to an absolutely wonderful therapist provided through Parliament and it has helped me so very much. I may not have been suicidal but I needed to talk. I needed to decompress with someone who didn't know me and for whom I did not have to return the favour. My therapist has helped me talk through my ideas and actions, and you are never the same person after cancer. Seeking counselling is just one of the best gifts I think you can give yourself.

Video diary: . . . Every day I've just had a drink, not a lot, just a wine maybe, yesterday was a Bailey's. But I tell you what . . . I wake up and I just feel like I want to be sobbing. I just want to be in a heap and sobbing. It's such a mental drain because you're thinking, On Friday, I could find out that I have breast cancer. My mum had breast cancer, my sister had breast cancer, my cousin died of breast cancer . . . Even though they said I haven't got the gene you just think, Oh, my God . . . I don't know . . . I think there needs to be something in place between you getting the phone call and the test for people because the emotional mental drain is killing. I think I'm eating my body weight through this week . . . Waiting for Friday is like pffff . . .

On 23 December, approximately ten days after my biopsy, I received another call from a withheld number. This time I was waiting to go into a dinner event. The person on the other line told me I needed to come in and see my surgeon the next day, and that was when I thought, *Well, I'm dying.*

'Surgeon?' I repeated. 'I've got a surgeon, so I've definitely got cancer. Are you telling me I've got cancer?' But

I was told that the surgeon only wanted to see me before going away on holiday, and they couldn't confirm the diagnosis on the phone. I went into the dinner with the weight of the news on my shoulders, knowing I needed surgery.

First thing the next day, I made my way to the hospital. I was convinced I was dying and only had twenty-four hours to live: a next-day appointment seemed serious. When the nurse came to collect me, she looked up and down the corridor and asked if I was by myself. Because of Covid, I had not been allowed to bring anyone with me to other appointments, so I thought this would be the same. It wasn't – but even so, I hardly told anyone. The nurse then turned to the surgeon inside a room and said, 'She's outside but she's by herself.' *I can hear you,* I thought, as well as, *Shit, I really must be dying*, and had my tissues at the ready as I sat down, prepared for the bad news.

The surgeon – who was this no-nonsense, straight-to-the-point woman – told me I had a DCIS (ductal carcinoma in situ) which is 0–1 stage breast cancer. 'If you have breast cancer, this is the best type to have,' she said. I really liked her approach but after the words 'You've got cancer,' you don't hear a lot more.

Almost immediately I was trying to concentrate on our conversation about checking my lymph nodes for cancer, cutting the bad cells out of my breast, and next steps. It was a lot of information to take in, and through the haze of wondering if I was going to die, I kind of just blanked out. She then asked me lots of questions about my sister, who had breast cancer. I didn't know the answers, but as I picked up my phone to check with her, I realized I hadn't told her. I went into another room and called her from there. It was tough. I composed myself, started speaking when she answered, and then I just broke down. My sister started crying too, although she didn't know why as I hadn't managed to get the words out.

My sister's breast-cancer journey was very emotional, and I imagine it was triggering for her that day to hear my news. Her situation was very close to being fatal and exemplified how Black women's voices and concerns are dismissed in our healthcare systems.

Unlike myself, my sister felt a lump in her breast, and immediately went to her GP, who told her not to worry. This happened a few more times – my sister going in, the GP sending her away – until she was in so much pain her husband took her to A&E, where they discovered she had advanced breast cancer. Her surgeons operated quickly, and my sister endured rounds of chemo- and radiotherapy. To get through such a difficult time, I took to pen and paper, writing her a long poem, something I used to do when I was feeling overwhelmed, or when I wanted to give someone a present. I used to ask people to tell me about a situation or a person, and then I would write for them, so this is what I did for her. Thank God, in the end, all was okay.

Her doctors were apologetic but, much like my drawer of police apologies, their words were insufficient to erase the trauma they had caused. If my sister had been listened to, respected and taken seriously, her suffering could have been avoided, but once again it seemed systemic racism had reared its ugly head. According to Breast Cancer Now, although breast cancer incidence rates are higher in white women, women who are South Asian, Chinese, Black or of mixed race 'experience differences in breast screening attendance, the stage and age of diagnosis, survival outcomes, and experiences of care and treatment'.[1] Black women are almost twice as likely to present with advanced breast cancers and types of breast cancer for which there are fewer treatment options. They report that 'around 25 per cent of Black African women and 22 per cent of Black Caribbean women are diagnosed with stage 3 or stage 4 breast cancer at diagnosis in England. This compares to 13 per cent of white women.'[2]

When Black women are fobbed off by their GPs and return home thinking everything's fine until it's too late, it's a no-brainer as to why these statistics ring true. Systemic racism is playing one of many roles in the escalation of advanced cancer, quality of care and treatment, and survival rates. Black women, for example, are also more than four times more likely to die in pregnancy and childbirth than their white female counterparts,[3] so why is that? We are not listened to and we are not treated with the same consideration and care as our white counterparts, with detrimental effects on our health and wellbeing. I have fought (and still fight) to be heard and considered, to be treated equitably. I am not alone in this battle – and often I wonder, what will it take for us to be heard, and to be treated with compassion? There are times when dismantling or confronting systemic racism and unconscious bias literally boils down to life or death, and there is no better example of that than our healthcare systems.

Video diary: So today I got the news that I have breast cancer in my left breast. It's non-invasive, it's in a contained area, so they should be able to operate, and have it removed but now I'm one of the hundreds of thousands of people who have cancer. A lot to take in. A lot of tears. A lot of emotion. Watch this space.

My surgery was booked for February, and my sister was determined to attend all my appointments with me. It was humbling to know that she was going to be there when I needed her, despite her own awful experience. I went to some appointments with Mark, but some I had to attend on my own, and there were times when I felt anxious about being recognized. I have to say, it was a relief to wear a mask in public, push back my distinctive hair, and conceal my identity. But during one appointment, as I checked in at the front desk, I could sense that the receptionist had clocked my name and knew exactly who I was. Out of curiosity, she asked me to pull down my mask, wanting to know if I was *the* Dawn Butler, but I was determined to stay anonymous.

'Why?' I asked. Being miserable was not the lasting impression I wanted to give someone meeting me for the first time. I was feeling vulnerable, not my usual self, and the last thing I wanted was to engage in conversation during a difficult time.

'I need to see your face,' she said.

'No . . . Covid!' I responded, with a chuckle, trying to move the conversation on.

'Are you Dawn Butler?'

'I don't know what you mean.'

The receptionist looked unconvinced, but I was able to take my seat – at the back of the waiting room, just out of the way. Shortly after, the receptionist approached me to say, 'I just want to thank you for all the work you do. It's really appreciated.'

I replied, 'I want to thank *you* for all the work that you do.' And as embarrassing as that was, with everyone in the room turning to look at me, wondering who the hell I was, and me just wanting to disappear into a wall, it was kind of her to say that to me, and for me to know that someone appreciated my efforts. My diagnosis might have been all-consuming, but she reminded me to stay strong, and to hold on to my purpose when I felt discouraged or sad. I don't mean strong in the sense of ignoring or pushing down my pain – it needed to be felt. I mean strong in my conviction of who I was and what I was born to do.

In the lead-up to the surgery there were many decisions to make about my body and what it was going to look like afterwards. My breasts would not look the same. The breast cancer nurse had pictures of what different reconstructive options looked like, and after several photos, I asked, 'Haven't you got any pictures of Black women?' which, thankfully, they did. I had to choose what I wanted after my mastectomy: I could leave my chest flat, opt for reconstruction or an implant. I knew I didn't want to have an implant – even getting my ears pierced twice was an ordeal. I settled on reconstruction, where they take fat from your belly to build a breast. It's not like a tummy tuck, but to make myself feel better I told myself that was what I was having so I could eat whatever crap I wanted to up until then. I had McDonald's, KFC, everything. My credit card even got declined one time because I'd never used it on so much junk food. It was a bit embarrassing, but it was a stressful time and I found myself eating my feelings.

Right before my operation, I spoke to one of my surgeons, Dr Yildrim, who is the funniest man with the best bedside manner. I told him I was nervous about what a big surgery it was. He replied, 'What do you care? You'll be asleep. I'm the one doing all the hard work.' It was exactly what I needed to hear, and it was nice to know that I was in good hands. Being able to trust your surgeons and know that you have a good team around you makes all the difference when it comes to treatment and recovery.

Video diary: You know what this has been: this has been a lesson in how I deal with crisis. I mean I don't know how I feel. I just want to get it over and done with. I don't even want to think about it. I feel exhausted. I feel like shit. I feel like, oh, my God, it's been three months. I just want to get it out. I don't even know how I feel. I have no feelings apart from praying and hoping that everything goes well – that's the most prominent feeling, just, let's get through this to face tomorrow. Thank you for all the love and support, and for everybody that loves me in my life. I'm forever grateful for that love.

Video diary: Hey everybody. I'm at the hospital. This is my room . . . just waiting to see the consultant and everything. I will keep you all updated. I'll see you when I come out from the other side. Love you all. Bye.

The operation took ten hours. Afterwards, one of my surgeons waited by my bedside when I woke up to tell me it had been a success, but I was out of it. I was in intensive care for three days and was in a lot of pain. I wanted to get up and walk, but I couldn't – my legs weren't working, and it took a while for my normal bodily functions to return. In this period, I also found out that when they removed the cancer cells, they'd found additional ones underneath. If it had been left untreated, it would have developed into a very invasive cancer.

Video diary: So, it's been a rough couple of days in hospital. They've taken out all of my cannulas [. . .]. People say [. . .] when you come out and you've had a cancer removed, what do you think about? Obviously, I'm pleased that my cancer has been removed [but] the doctors and nurses are doing an amazing job, and you think, I can't listen to their stories and not take action in a position like mine . . . so there's a couple of campaigns we're going to pursue about cancer care. The government has made an announcement; I'm going to read through it carefully . . . also, the BMI, the body mass index . . .

Even in my hospital bed, it was important for me to keep going, to keep fighting the good fight. It's how I choose to recharge my batteries when they're running low, so for me, focusing my energies on important issues and how to change them for the better makes me feel useful. The body mass index (BMI) struck me as something that desperately needed changing – I still wasn't heeding Paul Kenny's advice to pick my battles, but I couldn't get my mind off the BMI, even while I was recovering. On the surface, BMI doesn't overtly scream of bias, but when you consider that everyone is still being judged by the archaic measurements of a white male body mass, there's a problem, especially when it prevents people from receiving certain kinds of treatment and care.

I recall one of the first times I had a full medical check-up. After examining me, the GP looked at his chart and said, rather matter of fact, that I was obese. Given I was a curvy size 12 at the time with no fat to speak of, I was utterly shocked by this seemingly bizarre statement. The GP looked at me and back at his chart and said, 'Well, according to this you're actually very obese.' He was so confused by what his chart was telling him that he even called the nurse in and asked her to double-check his calculation.

I didn't know then how important a consideration BMI is when doctors or other medical professionals make clinical decisions. I was told by one of many clinicians that they could be prevented from staging timely medical interventions for their patients if they were classed as seriously obese. Patients are prevented from having certain surgeries, some of them life-changing, because of their BMI, a measuring system that hasn't changed or evolved.

You may think the BMI concept was created by a doctor, given its widespread acceptance in healthcare systems all over the world – but you would be wrong. It was created by astronomer and mathematician Adolphe Quetelet in the 1800s. Quetelet was on a quest to catalogue and identify *l'homme moyen* – a.k.a. the average man – in statistical terms. To do this he looked at the weight of lots of men and used that to determine what the average or otherwise ideal weight was. The issue? He measured only European men. Just over seven thousand, to be precise.

Of course, there was a huge flaw in his plan: we all come in different shapes and sizes – what is right for one person is not for another. It also means that the system of BMI isn't medically fit to determine what is or is not a healthy weight for a woman or an Asian man, for example.

As I lay in bed, it wasn't just the BMI system that was troubling me but the state of the NHS. I, along with so many other patients, was getting a behind-the-scenes look at its dismantling through the government's lack of investment, and it was heartbreaking. The staff were clearly under enormous pressure brought on by the pandemic, and they were dealing with a pile-up of patients who couldn't be seen or treated during the lockdowns. I had made many connections with the hardworking doctors and nurses throughout my journey so far, all of whom were giving it their all, and I felt I needed to say or do something, when I could. These people had saved my life, had looked after me when I was vulnerable and low, and they had all made sure that I was as comfortable as I could be during the scariest moments of my life. When I returned to the hospital after a terrible post-surgery infection, I saw the chaos first-hand.

Video diary: This is me looking better after being rushed back with an infection . . . and really the [hospital] needs to be closed because it is completely full. There's no staff and they are struggling. I am looking in their eyes and these doctors and nurses are struggling. There's nobody to take my bloods all day. I need my bloods to be taken to see if the infection markers have gone down, but there's only two nurses that can currently take my bloods, so the hospital needs to declare an emergency, but I don't think politically . . . I think the government's stopping them. I don't know what's going on but obviously I'm going to try and do something about it. Today for the first time I feel well enough to do what I can, to do something about it, so yeah . . . it's . . . um . . . yeah . . . the government are bastards. What are they doing to the NHS? And also, what are they doing to the staff? It's not fair what these people have gone through . . . [they're going through] PTSD and they're trying their best to manage a system that the government is trying to fail. It's cruel, man . . . this government is cruel . . . Anyway, I feel well . . . Hey, hey, I'm better!

Between the procedures and my recovery, everything in my life came to a halt. I was so used to being on the go, to being a workaholic, that to be forced to stop suddenly and slow down took me off guard. But that is what illness does to us. It provides a different level of focus and makes us assess our mortality. I became more reflective and turned inward. I had to take everything slowly, even when it came to walking and speaking. I guess you could say I was being more mindful, and it made me see life from a different perspective.

Eventually I took some time away from Parliament and spent several months recuperating to gather my strength and heal. The acts of care, love and kindness that came my way were overwhelming. People visited, delivered food and even arranged for someone to clean my house. I received lots and lots of wonderful flowers – although the florist nicked a bunch, as seen on my CCTV, so if I never thanked you, please know that was the reason! It was incredible to feel the amount of love that was out there for me, and to know that people were wishing me well, instead of ill.

The recovery process forced me to come to terms with

the lack of care I had for myself. It taught me that to be of service to others I had to learn to be of service to myself. I had to consider my own needs and desires, and I had to let go of the idea of sacrificing myself for the sake of others. There have been times in my life where I have not considered myself as much as I should, or I have failed to put myself first, but to be of good service it is important to have a good personal foundation, and to have a solid balance between work and life. It took a therapist to tell me that it was okay not to work 24/7 and that I could take time off to recharge my batteries. My therapist encouraged me to work smarter and more efficiently and helped me to identify the things I now want to achieve, making sure that I was surrounded by the right people to help me. I am prioritizing for the bigger picture now, especially as my energy levels change. I have learned to reserve my strength, and to say no to more things, or at least to know what my capacity is.

If you have survived cancer, you'll know you were a different person before you had it than you are afterwards. Your outlook completely changes, which changes your relationship to others and yourself. I've found my relationship to my body is not what it used to be: that has shifted too. I was terrified when I heard I would lose a breast. I couldn't wrap my head around the news, and it was the last thing I wanted. I had to convince myself that I was not defined by my body or my breasts, and it took time to come to terms with that.

My decision to have a reconstruction came from not wanting anything foreign in my body, but another woman I spoke to opted for implants. She felt her body had let her down, and she didn't like the idea of taking another part of it and putting it into her breast. We all have our own journey when it comes to accepting our bodies, and for me, post-cancer, nothing sums up how I feel better than the song 'This Is Me' from the theatre production *The Greatest Showman* (written by Keala Settle).

My scars represent a hard time in my life, but they are a part of me, so I'm learning to love them and not be ashamed of them. It takes time to love our bodies: there is so much we dislike and want to transform about them, and our bodies are always changing, from puberty through to adulthood and old age. It is a never-ending conversation and one that we continually have to strive to make peace with. But I love my body now. I have a whole new holiday wardrobe and a stomach so flat I'm thinking of getting a belly button piercing!

We should never be embarrassed to talk about our bodies or what happens to them. Breast cancer affects everybody – men, women, trans men, trans women, and non-binary people. My experiences inform my activism, and if something happens to me, I always want to make it better or easier for the next person coming behind me, no matter what it is.

When I felt ready to work again, my focus went on campaigning for breast-cancer awareness. I started small, at first speaking to a few good friends, like Kanya King, who mentioned ignoring their mammogram appointments. I gently reminded them of what had happened to me and that it could happen to them too. Due to Covid, Breast Cancer Now estimates that there are around a million women who haven't gone for their mammogram screening. They also believe that as many as eight thousand women are living with undiagnosed breast cancer in the UK because of the disruption caused by the pandemic and the underfunding of the NHS.

After my own experience, I wanted to give back, and decided to co-launch a campaign with the *Metro* called 'A Million Missing Mammograms' to find the million women and implore them to get screened. The reaction to the launch was so positive – #FindTheMillion had so many supportive comments. And, most importantly, I received so many emails and social-media messages from people who have either booked appointments as a result of seeing my campaign or have shared it to raise awareness with others. These people might not have made appointments otherwise, and plenty more would have done it without telling me, and it makes me feel good to know I've made a difference. After all, the earlier people catch this disease the better their chances are.

A mammogram saved my life, and I am grateful to have come through to the other side. I recently took my mum with me on a visit to Whipps Cross Hospital and she was so proud, showing off to the doctors that her daughter is an MP. One doctor looked at me, looked at the name, and said, 'Are you the one who told people to go for their mammograms? Thank you.' Big differences can happen through small actions. Taking on the under-funding of the NHS is a huge task and taking on cancer is an even bigger one – these things need heaps of man-power and resources – but helping just one woman catch breast cancer early is enough. Even when we don't think we're making a difference, we probably are.

Sometimes you read about people and the pain they have been through, and you think, How can they still advocate around the same issues? How can they advocate for safer driving when they have lost a loved one in a road accident, or how can the amazing Mina Smallman talk to police when two officers took pictures of her daughters' dead bodies? We all have our journeys, and some are filled with more tragedy than others. When I speak to women like Mina, I am given strength beyond belief.

Mina and I became close after what happened to her daughters, and when I was waiting to be called in about my results in hospital, not wanting to speak to anyone, she was phoning me relentlessly. I didn't want to pick up, but in the end, I did. Her first words were 'Dawn, what's wrong?' And that was it: I was in tears as I told her about waiting for the results of my biopsy. I told her I was sit-ting there alone, and she said, 'You are never alone. God is with you.' Those words guided me and made me feel safe at a time when I needed it most.

Every one of us can use our adversity to power change – but only if we so choose and only when we are able to do so. It's like being on a plane and the flight attendant telling passengers to put on their oxygen masks before helping others. I believe we all have a purpose, even if we don't think we do, and in order to find it, we need to slow down and examine who we are in detail. Working out where we often place our attention can be a good start. And sometimes advocating for someone else helps us make sense of the struggle we are experiencing in our own lives, giving us more insight, power and control. Our own experiences can shine a light on what we should be shouting about (or, at least, be talking about) to inspire real and sustainable change in a more collective and caring way.

9

THE LIME-GREEN SUIT

As I mentioned earlier, every year I try to have a theme to grow into and embrace. This year it's about the lime-green trouser suit I recently bought. When I walk into a room full of grey suits and they see me in lime green, some people in that room will be thinking: *Oh, my God, what the hell is she wearing? How can someone be wearing a lime-green suit when we are a grey-suit establishment? We have always worn grey suits. Our customers expect us to be in grey suits. We cannot have this lime-green suit person coming in and upsetting the status quo.* But because I consider myself a disruptor, and have fully owned this quality within myself, I will ignore those people and focus my attention on the few in the room who have a growth mindset, those who will question and be curious about why I've turned up in a lime-green suit.

They will wonder what I'm trying to say with the lime-green suit and will consider what else they can learn from my approach. There will also be at least one person in the room who will think: *I really like that lime-green suit. I don't think I could wear it, but I really like it.* This person will most likely be appreciative of my boldness and thank me later for what I've done, perhaps whispering their gratitude outside the room so as not to expose themselves in a room full of grey suits. And the next day, this person might come to work wearing a colourful tie because I opened the door for them with my lime-green suit. They will think: *This is good ... This is a bit of me. I'm not going to go mad with a lime-green suit, but I'll certainly start here.*

Change happens when we are more fully in touch with who we are. It takes one person to be bold to allow others to follow suit. As a disruptor, I have understood that I will not always be liked and that's okay. I love my lime-green suit, so I'm not going to have someone tell me they hate it and take that to heart. *It's okay if you don't like it, but I do — you didn't buy it. It's mine and I like it. That's why I bought it, and that's why I'm wearing it.*

We cannot have people creating doubt within us as to who we are or what decisions we choose to make. Instead, it's important to stand strong and with conviction, not just for us, but for those around us who need that too. We need to show companies and organizations that someone who turns up in a lime-green suit can still do their job well, and will perhaps bring even more to the table. The last thing any of us wants is for you to look at your wardrobe and choose the grey suit, when deep down it's lime green that you really want to wear. No one wants to start their day depressed on the train, wishing they could've worn their lime-green suit!

The lime-green suit is about growing into your authenticity to discover your true purpose, if you don't already know it. It's about bringing your truest self to the workplace, to school, to church, or to any endeavour you choose. How can you stop making yourself small just to appease others? How can you amplify your light, gaining the strength to advocate for yourself and others? How can you bring more of your own lime-green suit into the everyday?

The lime-green suit is about finding our people and inspiring others, because alongside deepening a stronger relationship with ourselves, it's paramount that we find others who can share in and enhance our magic. We are strongest when we have allies. This is a positive rallying cry. There is power in numbers, and nothing is more gratifying than knowing that other people are on your side. If I had known that my own party would initially abandon me when I called Boris Johnson a liar, I would have asked a few MPs to come and sit with me so that I felt supported and comforted. We call this 'doughnutting' in Parliament – when a person giving a maiden or emotional speech is surrounded by fellow MPs for extra reinforcement.

If you are considering going out on a ledge, one that might be risky, have a think about the people you can approach to say, 'Look, I'm going to do this thing, and it might go wrong, or I might need some help. Can you back me up? Or how can you help me?' Having others to champion your causes and to absorb the shock of a potential aftermath is not only great for your mental health, but it also makes you feel more courageous.

As the MP for Brent Central, I have to own who I am with every fibre of my being as the representative of one of the most diverse constituencies in the UK. It allows me to build solid relationships with the institutions that exist within my constituency, and to make sure they're working as effectively as possible. Because I know how scary it is for individuals to speak up against seniority or the system, I encourage people, like my local police officers, nurses and doctors, to whistle-blow to me if there's an insurmountable issue they can't handle on their own. I use my position to allow others to trust that I will advocate on their behalf and confidentially.

We are all interconnected, whether we like it or not, which is why every single constituent in Brent matters to me, whether they voted for me or not. I am still their MP. Just the other day a constituent's husband died – a wonderful musician; I once met him and he gave me a CD. On my way to Parliament, I went to visit her, first writing her a letter that I planned to post through her letterbox. When I got there, I decided to knock to see if she was in, and when she answered the door, she was stunned to see me standing there. I gave her my deepest condolences and we had a brief chat before I went on my way. My visit meant a lot to her, but that moment of connection and community meant a lot to me too. How can we look after each other a bit more? She is just one of thousands of constituents, but each moment shared with the people I represent, whether it be to celebrate a festival, attend a park run or luncheon or mourn a loss, it all matters.

When there are tragedies in Brent, big or small, I take it very personally. When something good happens, I'm promoting the hell out of it, and when something bad happens, I'm doing what I need to do to try to solve our problems. When I first came into Brent, we had a violent incident, on average, every seven days, and I made it my mission to make Brent safer. Obviously, I couldn't physically take every weapon off the streets, but I was determined to protect my constituents as much as possible. I started working with the local police and community leaders. We all sat around a table and talked out the nuances of the issues and how we could tackle them, what part we each could play to resolve some of the issues that were in our control. And it worked – I remember a summer where there were no fatal incidents. It was a strong example of the 'village' coming together to keep our streets safe. There was confidence in the trust that was built across sectors, and it was fairness and understanding that yielded that result.

The other thing I wanted to do was to combat people's negative biases of Brent. As my brothers taught me long ago, words matter, and we should never allow people to define or label us or confine us to their own limited or bigoted beliefs. When I went on TV to discuss a shooting, for example, I made sure that I counteracted such horrible news with something positive that outweighed the negative, because often presenters or guests wanted to concentrate on portraying Brent as a 'bad' place, when so many wonderful things happen there as well. Someone once compared Brent to the West Baltimore depicted in the American police drama *The Wire* (they were saying that Brent was a place afflicted by criminality, drugs and poverty), and I was livid, thinking, *You're not going to paint my Brent that way*. Part of being a disruptor or wearing that lime-green suit entails controlling your own narratives and defining yourself for yourself.

It all boils down to people being scared of what they don't know. We saw this during Brexit, for example, and our government still tries to use refugees as the latest scapegoat to further their aims to stoke a fake culture war. But people who come to Brent can always find a home where they're accepted. This is one of the things I like to celebrate about Brent: the robustness of our community.

One year a racist organization came to the constituency and filmed outside a mosque after Friday prayers. They were trying to paint Muslims as 'taking over the country' and they interviewed locals to get people to express hate. But instead people were saying things like, 'It's only an hour on a Friday. They're only going to say their prayers, then go back to work. It's not much of an inconvenience.' And someone else said something like 'My neighbour's Muslim and they're really nice. They look after my cat when I'm away.' The organization tried their hardest to sow divisions within the community, but people were so used to having neighbours who were

Muslim, West Indian, African, Irish, Eastern European, Jewish, you name it, that they failed. More than 170 languages are spoken in Brent, so people were like, *What are you talking about? That's not my lived experience of my community, so you leave. We don't want you here.*

This is why I implore people to take themselves out of their comfort zones. The more you learn or experience, the more barriers you break down and through, the more you stop fearing everything and everyone. Once you appreciate that someone can wear a lime-green suit and see the beauty in that, you will see the beauty in a bright orange or deep magenta suit.

We need to train people to treat us as we want to be treated. This starts on a personal level, and it extends to a collective level. We have no control over other people's actions, but we can change how they treat us through our own reactions: if someone is behaving poorly towards us and we accept that behaviour without challenging it, pretending nothing happened and everything is okay, that person will treat us poorly again. If, instead, we say to the person that what they did was not okay, or let them know how it made us feel, next time they will alter how they treat us.

To push this further, as a collective, if we allow the government to strip us of our rights – the right to protest, the right to vote, the right to decent pay – they will stop at nothing to shut all of us down. Just as we must train people to treat us as we want to be treated, we must also train our systems and structures to do the same. We are

seeing the rise of protests in this country as people understand they have personal power. They are piping up and
saying, 'We don't want to be treated like this any more.
We should be able to afford to live, to eat, to be kept
warm.' Why do you think the government, which usually takes ages to put through any legislation that makes
a difference to the lives of many, suddenly wants to rush
through the anti-trade-union Bill in a matter of weeks?
They are simply protecting themselves and their interests, and if we continue with business as usual, they will
continue to strip away our power until we are left with
very little agency. Therefore, we cannot stop. We must
keep fighting. And I hope this book has given you the
tools to do so.

AFTERWORD

THE LAST THING I WANT to do is provide you with a playlist of some of the most inspirational songs that I have clung to throughout my life because there can be no revolution without music or joy.

https://open.spotify.com/playlist/1LF6eeOFonBxoQE
RhzEaaG?si=GKN2KYxiST6pesotnlZCsg&dd=1

'Silly Games', Janet Kay
'Hard Times', Pablo Gad
'Three Little Birds', Bob Marley and the Wailers
'Optimistic', Sounds of Blackness
'Apparently Nothin'', Young Disciples
'Sexy Cinderella', Lynden David Hall

'Body Fusion', Starvue
'Sensitivity', Ralph Tresvant
'Yo That's a Lot a Body', Ready for the World
'Oasis', Helen Baylor
'There's Nothing Like This', Omar
'Can We Talk', Tevin Campbell
'Just Fine', Mary J. Blige
'I'm So Into You', SWV
'Every Little Step', Bobby Brown
'Stay', Jodeci
'Juicy', The Notorious B.I.G.
'If I Ruled the World (Imagine That)',
Nas, Ms Lauryn Hill
'I'll Be There For You/You're All I Need to Get By',
Method Man, Mary J. Blige
'Ex-Factor', Ms Lauryn Hill
'This Is Me', Keala Settle, The Greatest Showman
Ensemble
'(Something Inside) So Strong', Labi Siffre, Kevin
W. Smith
'Here and Now', Luther Vandross
'You Are Not Alone', Emeli Sandé
'I Should've Known Better', Mica Paris
'Dreams', Gabrielle
'Fallen Soldier', Beverley Knight
'Feel So High', Des'ree
'Back to Life', Soul II Soul, Caron Wheeler
'No More', Jamelia
'Long Hard Road', Sade

'Another Lifetime', Nao
'Pain', Ms Dynamite
'Grace Under Pressure', Eternal
'F**kin' Perfect', P!nk
'Salute', Little Mix
'Perfect', Anne-Marie
'Eternal Light', Free Nationals, Chronixx
'Black', Dave
'Tightrope', JLS
'Breakeven', The Script
'9 to 5', Dolly Parton
'Key to the World', Rudy Thomas
'I'm So Sorry', Carroll Thompson
'Together At Last', Alexis Ffrench, Jobim Ffrench
'Candy', Cameo
'Rastaman Live Up', Bob Marley and The Wailers
'Still I Rise', Carroll Thompson
'When Doves Cry', Prince
'Kissing You', Keith Washington
'Talkin' Bout A Revolution', Tracy Chapman
'I Don't Feel Noways Tired', James Cleveland
'Black Pride', Kofi

ACKNOWLEDGEMENTS

Thank you to Luc, Lee, Pat, Cammille, Sean, Gary and Mark for helping me edit this book. Also to Lady Lynda, Sadiq, Chris and Paul Boeteng, your help has been invaluable, and to Jennifer Obidike for helping me say what I want to say.

In Brent, there are many different communities, and over 170 languages spoken. I've learned so much from all of them. Also, thanks to the religious institutions: churches, mosques, temples, Mandirs, Synagogues, and all who have prayed for me.

All the West Indian, Indian, Greek and other restaurants who have kept us fed over the years.

Leanne, Jan, Paulette, Dawn, Linda, Kelly, Carmel, Anjula, Ali, Guna, Akala, thank you.

Leigh-Ann Pinnock, it's been a joy to help you find your purpose – keep shining. Adele (Emeli Sandé), I feel that your purpose is bigger than you can imagine.

To my friends from school and college who keep me grounded, you know who you are. To my Labour family, let's win the next election with a purpose for a fairer and equitable society. And, of course, to my family, my extended family, and my in-laws.

There are so many more I could thank, but I'd be here all day.

APPENDIX

As I mentioned in the 'Driving While Black' chapter, I had a considerable amount of correspondence with the Metropolitan Police about my traffic stop. I knew I'd have to fight hard to get to the truth, and I carefully considered and responded to every single point that their review of the circumstances around the stop raised. This was tiring work, but I want to show how diligent and relentless we all need to be to force change. Here, for the first time, are my notes on their findings, which helped me formulate my responses.

OFFICER 1 is the male officer, in the first unmarked car, who removed the keys from the ignition.

OFFICER 2 is the female officer in the first unmarked car.

OFFICER 3 is another male officer in the first unmarked car.

OFFICER 4 is the male officer in the first unmarked car who questioned me on the passenger side about where we were going.

OFFICER 5 is the female officer who arrived in the marked car.

METROPOLITAN POLICE'S REVIEW LETTER	MY RESPONSES
'In order to properly address the issues, the following material was obtained and reviewed: OFFICER 1's Body Worn Video (BWV) footage dated 9th August 2020.'	Was there only one BWV available? Are vehicles used for traffic stops not fitted with cameras? How many police cars doing vehicle stops are fitted with cameras?
OFFICER 2 says: 'I shouted out the registration of the vehicle.' OFFICER 1 says, 'The phonetic alphabet was not used.'	Is it standard practice to use phonetics? If so why was this not used? The car was driving at approximately 5 m.p.h. as we were approaching traffic lights, so there would have been plenty of time to use the phonetic alphabet.
OFFICER 1 says: 'I conducted a check on this registration ... and noticed the vehicle was registered to North Yorkshire. I confirmed the colour was silver but did not confirm the make, model of the vehicle or VRM.'	Is it standard practice to stop people because of the colour of a car? What is the standard training for vehicle stops? How long have these officers been assigned to vehicle-stop duties?
OFFICER 2 says: 'Upon being made aware the vehicle was registered to an address in Yorkshire, [I] activated the vehicles lights and sirens.'	Why was Yorkshire a cause for suspicion? Should this not have to be combined with something else (driving erratically or some other suspicious activity?) Can people not travel?
'Based on the misapprehension your friend's vehicle was not registered locally, OFFICER 2 decided the vehicle would be stopped.'	Why was this a valid reason? Would they apply this reasoning anywhere? Or is it location-dependent?

OFFICER 2 says: 'In ordinary times, [the fact the vehicle wasn't registered locally] would lead me to further enquiries with the driver to enquire why the vehicle was in London. (My considerations were possible county lines activity or a cloned/stolen vehicle being used in crime).'	Is this seriously used as a valid reason? Is this good policing? Surely you need more grounds than this.
'OFFICER 3 did not remain by your friend's vehicle as he did not wish to draw adverse interest in the stop from members of the public.'	At least two police officers were constantly with us. Flashing lights were surrounding the car. People were slowing down and looking so it seemed like it was a really big bust. If this is the interpretation, there is a disconnect from the reality of the situation. Also, the detail in this letter confirms the high level of police activity during this incorrect stop.
'OFFICER 5 has no recollection of the stop.'	Which car was this? Are they not required to take note of things like this?
'The accounts by OFFICER 1, OFFICER 2 and OFFICER 3 state that the rear window tint of your friend's vehicle was what initially drew their attention.'	Why? It is a standard factory-made tint, and the car was purchased that way.
OFFICER 2: '[A rear window tint] is often used as a way of concealing identity of the occupants and I therefore requested further information on the vehicle.'	This is a very biased assumption. This is pre-judging and not good policing. What is the percentage of vehicles in the UK with tinted windows?

OFFICER 3: 'My attention was drawn . . . due to the heavily tinted rear windows.'	They are factory legal standard. Are police trained to identify illegal tints?
OFFICER 3: '[Tinted windows are] sometimes a tactic used by gang members.'	So the assumption was that there were gang members in the vehicle? This is classic dangerous group-think. How often are tinted windows used as a tactic? Are there police statistics on this? How many BMWs are stopped by police? What are the statistics of stops by make, model, tinted windows? Can we conclude that if anyone drives a BMW with factory-standard tinted windows that the Metropolitan Police will deem them possible drug dealers?
OFFICER 1 and OFFICER 5's vehicles 'were not equipped with dashboard-mounted cameras.'	Were any police vehicles fitted with a camera that day?
OFFICER 2 explains: 'A marked vehicle joined them at the stop and she informed the driver that their presence was not required and they could leave.'	How many vehicles in total were passing? And how did they know about the stop?

'OFFICER 4 did not record the incident on BWV because his battery was not charged.'	What is the police procedure? Are they required to be used? Do BWV batteries need to be charged before starting a shift? Is it not someone's responsibility to do this? And if it's acceptable not to have one charged, does this not leave it open to misuse? Could an officer not deliberately fail to charge it or use this as an excuse for not using it? This is bad practice. Is there a way to charge batteries in the car? What sort of batteries do BWV use?
'OFFICER 4 believes only two vehicles were involved in the stop.'	Which two vehicles? What do they take to mean as 'involved'?
'OFFICER 1 approached your friend, established the details he provided did not match the details shown for the vehicle.'	Well, if the only thing they checked was the silver colour of the car, it isn't really good policing.
OFFICER 1's emails clarify 'details of other officers present'.	Who are they?
'OFFICER 1's radio transmission data does not show any activity' between the times for the stop.	Was this the only person having any radio contact? What were the other officers doing at that time? I observed at least three officers speaking behind us.

'OFFICER 2's statement is incorrectly dated.'	Attention to detail is vital in policing – the incorrect procedures that seem to have been used indicate a pattern and the need for training.
'OFFICER 1 believed your friend's vehicle to be registered in Yorkshire, it is not entirely clear why this led him to have concerns regarding whether the vehicle was properly insured.'	Transparent and intelligent policing is important if we are to build trust between the police and us citizens.
'OFFICER 1 states he did not notice that the make and model of the vehicle shown on PNC did not match that of the vehicle.'	It would seem that if police are on vehicle-stop duty this is the very thing they should be noticing. It would be good to know what training is given and what skills are needed to do the job. Please remember that the vehicle was travelling at less than 5 m.p.h. approaching traffic lights. Is it not vital to check the details before making a decision to stop? Especially in a non-urgent case as this?
OFFICER 1's statement says: 'There was no way of seeing who was in the car due to the rear-tinted window.'	Are wing mirrors ever used to see who is driving a car? Also, could you explain what difference to decision-making it would make to be able to see who is inside?

'OFFICER 1's BWV shows that when your friend's vehicle was stopped it was ahead of the police vehicle. The evidence is consistent with the officers' accounts that the police vehicle was behind you and the rear window tints would have obscured the officers' vision of you and your friend.'	Where were the other vehicles positioned that were involved in the stop?
'During the stop, you [Dawn] made reference to OFFICER 1 profiling "people who are driving a certain type of car". OFFICER 1's attention was not drawn to the vehicle arbitrarily . . . [Tinted windows] is one of the indicators that sparks the professional curiosity of officers tasked specifically with tackling gang crime.'	What is the name for stopping a vehicle because of the make and tinted windows? Surely the tinted windows are either at an illegal level, and there are grounds for a stop, or you don't stop at all. Is there training on this?
'You may be aware of the recent MPS pilot to record the ethnicity of motorists stopped in London.'	Excellent pilot. Are there any data/ statistics from the pilot?
'In the BWV, OFFICER 1 appears convinced that there was a PNC error from the first check in showing the vehicle registered outside the local area. In his statement, OFFICER 1 accepts the error was his.'	This is accepted. We all make mistakes.
OFFICER 1 says: 'As I looked at my laptop I realized the vehicle PNC [the police database which stores vehicle records] was not on screen.'	Why was that? Can the process be explained to me?

'I am able to confirm there were three police cars present.'	Where were these cars positioned? Did they all have their sirens on? Did any have dash cams? Were there any communications between the three cars?
'It just so happened that a marked police unit pulled up behind our police vehicle during the stop.'	Please confirm that this was the same police vehicle that was in front of us. Is there any appreciation or understanding of the stress, anxiety and embarrassment that this type of police attention causes?
'I am satisfied that OFFICER 5 was travelling in the opposite direction . . .'	Can it be explained in more detail how this works and how other police vehicles get involved? Did OFFICER 5 put on the warning lights too?
'OFFICER 2 informed the driver [of the marked vehicle] their presence was not required.'	Was this the car that was in front of us? What was the conversation? How many police officers were in each car?
OFFICER 2 says: 'A further unmarked vehicle from my team who had taken the same route to [the area they were patrolling] also pulled up to see if we needed anything.'	There are lots of police cars here – how does this work? Also why was the deputy police commissioner not told about the other two cars that were present before he wrote his statement?
'I do not consider it proportionate to examine the transmission data for the radios.'	How do we learn the lessons if we don't consider all the facts?

'OFFICER 1 and OFFICER 5 state their respective vehicles were not equipped with dashboard mounted cameras.'	So, none of the police vehicles out on vehicle stops had dashboard cameras?
'Officers stopping vehicles may decide to record the stop on Compute Aided Despatch (CAD) as it is happening. The reason for this is to make local units aware of the activity so that, in the event of assistance being required, units can be efficiently deployed to offer support. On this occasion the stop was not recorded.' OFFICER 2 says: 'I did not place a vehicle stop CAD . . . We do this when there is an officer safety risk which there was not in this circumstance.'	Why would the other police cars stop if it wasn't recorded on the CAD system?
OFFICER 1 says: 'I was using common law to remove the keys . . . I believed that the driver may have been uninsured and I wanted to prevent any harm occurring to any other members of the public, myself or my colleagues as he was an unknown risk.'	This is a contradiction to the CAD statement above about there not being an officer safety risk. Please explain. For background information: there is an issue with the police and the perception of risk and harm caused by Black men. For instance, handcuffing is often used before asking any questions when stopping and searching.

'OFFICER 1's decision to take the ignition keys was not incorrect in principle . . . The available material does not provide objective reasons to support his decision. OFFICER 1 and his colleagues do not demonstrate any concern at your or your friend's behaviour. That the second and third police vehicles were directed to leave is inconsistent with an apprehension that your friend may have driven off [. . .] [But] taking all factors into account . . . I conclude that OFFICER 1's action in securing the ignition keys was well-intentioned.'	I believe it was a perceived bias after seeing the colour of our skin, even though all the evidence pointed to the fact that we were not a risk. And I maintain that the conclusion that it was well-intentioned confirms there is an institutional issue.
'My review has been unable to identify any assumptions made by OFFICER 1 regarding you or your friend when he decided to remove the ignition keys'	My belief is that the whole report highlights the assumption. It is institutional, not an individual act. This is an important part of policing.
'It is my view that OFFICER 1 could have given greater consideration to how realistic the likelihood of the risks he identified actually occurring and balanced this against the likely impact of his actions on you and your friend. I am recommending he would benefit from the Reflective Practice Review Process.'	Not just OFFICER 1, but all of the officers involved could have given greater consideration to the risks. I consider there were a number of mistakes, assumptions and biases throughout this whole stop. I would be interested in understanding the Reflective Practice Review.

'That I have been unable to obtain any communication data between the three vehicles does not cause me concern. Of the two additional vehicles with peripheral involvement in the stop, one happened to be travelling in the opposite direction . . .'	This highlights that another vehicle was involved that the reviewer has yet to identify, as there was a police car in front of us.
'I apologize on behalf of the Metropolitan Police Service that your interaction with OFFICER 1 has left you upset with the service you received.'	It wasn't just OFFICER 1: the female police officer deliberately escalated the situation. What reflective practice would she be given? OFFICER 4, who spoke to me asking unnecessary questions, again escalated the situation. Of all the officers directly involved OFFICER 1 had the best communication skills.
'Throughout the handling of this complaint, we have carefully considered whether there are any opportunities for learning or improvement. Learning identified? No.'	Please see all of the above, I disagree that no opportunities for learning can be identified.

SOURCES

2. A GOOD TEACHER MAKES ALL THE DIFFERENCE

Break the cycle: ending school-to-prison pipelines in the UK – Breakthrough (https://www.wearebreakthrough.org/blog/break-the-cycle-ending-school-to-prison-pipelines-in-the-uk)

'We can't say that this is something in the past', British Psychological Society (https://www.bps.org.uk/psychologist/we-cant-say-something-past)

3. DRIVING WHILE BLACK

Excerpts from Dawn's essay 'Black British Politicians Matter' in *Black British Lives Matter*, Lenny Henry and Marcus Ryder, Faber & Faber, London, 2021

https://www.youtube.com/watch?v=bTPLOZiUxjo

https://www.theguardian.com/law/video/2020/aug/09/labour-mp-dawn-butler-films-herself-being-stopped-by-police-in-london-video

https://news.sky.com/story/labour-mp-dawn-butler-was-stopped-by-officers-because-of-human-error-metropolitan-police-says-12047518

https://www.theguardian.com/uk-news/2020/aug/12/senior-met-officer-defends-police-who-stopped-dawn-butler

https://www.lbc.co.uk/radio/presenters/shelagh-fogarty/good-officers-get-excommunicated-dawn-butler-on-broken-met-police/

https://www.theguardian.com/uk-news/2022/oct/11/met-to-stop-recording-ethnicity-of-drivers-stopped-by-its-officers

https://www.theguardian.com/uk-news/2021/jan/18/met-police-to-start-recording-ethnicity-of-people-stopped-in-cars

https://www.london.gov.uk/publications/action-plan-transparency-accountability-and-trust-policing

https://www.stop-watch.org

https://www.youtube.com/watch?v=M_pL9ZgDfDw

https://www.dawnbutler.org.uk/bibaa-nicole-joint-statement

https://metro.co.uk/2021/11/09/bibaa-and-nicole-deserved-so-much-better-a-sorry-doesnt-cut-it-15565684/

4. NOT YOUR NORMAL POLITICIAN

https://www.theguardian.com/commentisfree/2017/mar/17/british-sign-language-parliament-bsi-deaf-hard-hearing

https://nacy.ca/wp-content/uploads/2020/06/An_Agenda_for_Youth_Engagement_2009.pdf

https://trumpetmediagroup.com/the-trumpet/Passages/dame-betty-asafu-adjaye-tribute-to-a-tireless-woman-on-a/

5. NOBODY LIKES THE R-WORD

https://www.theguardian.com/media/2018/jan/03/toby-young-is-ideal-man-for-university-watchdog-says-boris-johnson

https://www.theguardian.com/media/2018/jan/07/toby-young-faces-fresh-calls-for-his-sacking-in-misogyny-row

https://www.independent.co.uk/news/people/black-mp-dawn-butler-reveals-she-was-victim-of-racism-in-parliament-after-fellow-mp-assumed-she-was-a-cleaner-a6901261.html

https://www.theguardian.com/world/2008/apr/13/race.houseofcommons

https://www.parliament.uk/about/mps-and-lords/members/mps/

https://www.parliament.uk/about/how/committees/

https://web.archive.org/web/20180827044104/http://www.thevisibilityproject.com/2014/05/27/on-moya-bailey-misogynoir-and-why-both-are-important/

6. WE ARE PHENOMENAL WOMEN

https://www.parliament.uk/globalassets/globalassets/proxyvotingscheme13oct2022.pdf

https://www.parliament.uk/globalassets/globalassets/explanatory-memorandum-by-the-clerk-of-the-house-on-the-motion-in-the-name-of-the-leader-of-the-house-relating-to-voting-by-proxy.pdf

https://committees.parliament.uk/publications/22837/documents/173562/default/

https://hansard.parliament.uk/commons/2022–10–12/debates/C7D486BC-7EF7–4AF5–8712-BA916FD56EA6/VotingByProxy(AmendmentAndExtension)

https://www.ealingtimes.co.uk/news/14212241.mp-accused-unconscious-racism-role-deputy-speaker/

https://pavilionlabour.wordpress.com/reports/elaine-bewley-reports/

https://www.youtube.com/watch?v=p6GCnt___to

https://www.thepinknews.com/2020/01/13/dawn-butler-labour-party-mp-deputy-leader-bid-gay-giraffes-gra-trans-rights/

https://www.thepinknews.com/2019/10/17/dawn-butler-gender-recognition-act-delay-pinknews-awards-labour-mp-community-group/

https://www.thepinknews.com/2019/11/20/dawn-butler-labour-transgender-gra-reform-women-equalities-minister-exclusive/

https://www.glamourmagazine.co.uk/article/dawn-butler-life-as-a-female-black-mp

https://labour.org.uk/press/black-history-british-history-jeremy-corbyn-says-schools-teach-black-british-history-empire-slavery/

https://labour.org.uk/press/dawn-butler-speaking-labour-party-conference/

https://www.youtube.com/watch?v=93yMJ3rjpqw

7. WHO'S THE LIAR NOW?

https://metro.co.uk/2020/02/14/im-running-deputy-leader-labour-party-12204676/

https://metro.co.uk/2019/11/07/dawn-butler-stand-labour-deputy-leader-tom-watsons-resignation-11064031/

https://labourlist.org/2020/01/hundreds-of-labour-members-urge-mps-to-put-dawn-butler-on-the-ballot-paper/

https://fabians.org.uk/wp-content/uploads/2021/10/FABJ9157-Fabian-review-Autumn-WEB-210915–4.pdf

https://metro.co.uk/2019/10/17/mp-dawn-butler-terrorised-tube-woman-threatened-kill-10936890/

https://www.dawnbutler.org.uk/peddie

https://metro.co.uk/2022/01/07/as-an-mp-ive-had-death-threats-and-been-attacked-i-wont-be-silenced-15881199/

https://www.youtube.com/watch?v=O2aafrWpsKg

https://edition.cnn.com/2019/07/23/africa/boris-johnson-africa-intl/index.html

https://twitter.com/snigskitchen/status/1235510503969079296

https://www.youtube.com/watch?v=aoG2R2zBsTw

https://www.dawnbutler.org.uk/dawn_spoke_at_the_ppe_contract_debate_calling_out_government_corruption

https://www.theguardian.com/society/2022/nov/13/controversial-360m-nhs-england-data-platform-lined-up-for-trump-backers-firm

https://www.theguardian.com/world/ng-interactive/2020/dec/16/covid-chaos-a-timeline-of-the-uks-handling-of-the-coronavirus-crisis

https://www.theguardian.com/news/2018/mar/17/cambridge-analytica-facebook-influence-us-election

https://twitter.com/DawnButlerBrent/status/1285655241627774981?s=19

https://www.independent.co.uk/news/uk/politics/dawn-butler-black-lives-matter-constituency-office-close-racism-a9610626.html

https://www.theguardian.com/society/2020/sep/15/ex-tory-mp-charlie-elphicke-jailed-for-two-years-for-sexual-assaults

8. THE BODY NEEDS REST

https://metro.co.uk/2022/07/30/dawn-butler-i-had-no-symptoms-when-i-was-diagnosed-with-breast-cancer-17086659/

https://metro.co.uk/2022/11/25/the-odds-are-already-stacked-against-black-women-with-cancer-17822875/

ENDNOTES

2. A GOOD TEACHER MAKES ALL THE DIFFERENCE

1   *Biased: The New Science of Race and Inequality*, Jennifer Eberhardt, William Heinemann, London, 2019
2   https://www.theguardian.com/education/2021/mar/24/exclusion-rates-black-caribbean-pupils-england
3   https://www.ymca.org.uk/wp-content/uploads/2020/10/ymca-young-and-black.pdf

3. DRIVING WHILE BLACK

1   Dr Martin Luther King Jr, 'Speech on Receipt of Honorary Doctorate in Civil Law', November 13, 1967, University of Newcastle upon Tyne
2   https://www.gov.uk/government/statistics/police-powers-and-procedures-stop-and-search-and-arrests-england-and-wales-year-ending-31-march-2022/police-powers-and-procedures-stop-and-search-and-arrests-england-and-wales-year-ending-31-march-2022
3   https://metro.co.uk/2020/08/08/black-people-should-not-scared-phone-police-when-need-help-13098631/
4   https://www.standard.co.uk/news/politics/boris-johnson-dawn-butler-police-stop-a4520776.html
5   https://www.facebook.com/metpoliceuk/photos/a.260071987383114/3325611067495842/?type=3

6   Dawn Butler (2020), Interview by Eamonn Holmes and Ruth
     Langsford, *This Morning*, ITV, 11 August 2020. https://www.
     youtube.com/watch?v=M_pL9ZgDfDw

7   https://www.stop-watch.org/what-we-do/research/traffic-
     stops-factsheet/

8   https://www.theguardian.com/law/2020/jul/08/
     one-in-10-of-londons-young-black-males-stopped-by-police-
     in-may

5. NOBODY LIKES THE R-WORD

1   https://commonslibrary.parliament.uk/research-briefings/
     sn01250/

2   https://www.independent.co.uk/news/people/black-mp-
     dawn-butler-reveals-she-was-victim-of-racism-in-
     parliament-after-fellow-mp-assumed-she-was-a-cleaner-
     a6901261.html

3   https://www.theguardian.com/politics/2019/oct/14/
     lib-dem-apologises-dawn-butler-lied-accounts-racism-
     westminster

4   https://twitter.com/dawnbutlerbrent/status/950456285702639618

5   https://www.spectator.co.uk/article/
     dawn-butler-spoiled-one-of-the-best-days-of-my-life/

6   https://twitter.com/dawnbutlerbrent/
     status/1030741609984548864

7   https://hansard.parliament.uk/commons/2010–03–10/
     debates/10031061000027/ICT(ExternalConsultants)

6. WE ARE PHENOMENAL WOMEN

1   https://www.standard.co.uk/news/politics/heavily-pregnant-
     mp-allegedly-told-she-was-bringing-down-whole-of-
     womankind-by-taking-snack-break-a3151686.html

2 https://kids.frontiersin.org/articles/10.3389/frym.2021.608843
3 https://www.huffingtonpost.co.uk/2015/09/17/jess-phillips-diane-abbott-corbyn_n_8151468.html
4 https://www.standard.co.uk/news/politics/labour-women-in-fight-for-top-job-a3343606.html
5 https://www.thepinknews.com/2019/11/20/dawn-butler-labour-transgender-gra-reform-women-equalities-minister-exclusive/
6 https://publications.parliament.uk/pa/cm201719/cmselect/cmwomeq/1470/147010.htm

7. WHO'S THE LIAR NOW?

1 https://labour.org.uk/press/crony-covid-contracts-hit-3-5bn-of-taxpayers-money/
2 https://www.kentonline.co.uk/sevenoaks/news/mps-dismay-at-sentence-for-bullet-to-the-head-tweet-262025/
3 Dawn Butler and Laura Trott (2020), Interview by Jo Coburn, *Politics Live*, BBC, 4 March 2020. https://www.indy100.com/politics/dawn-butler-calls-out-boris-johnson-racism-during-panel-debate-with-mp-laura-trott

8. THE BODY NEEDS REST

1 https://breastcancernow.org/about-us/media/facts-statistics/how-are-people-ethnically-diverse-backgrounds-impacted-breast-cancer
2 Ibid.
3 https://www.birthrights.org.uk/2021/11/11/new-mbrrace-report-shows-black-women-still-four-times-more-likely-to-die-in-pregnancy-and-childbirth/

Dawn Butler is the Labour MP for Brent Central and stands up for groups and people in society who are often under-represented. One of six children, she was born and raised in East London to expats from Jamaica. At a young age, she worked on a market stall as well as helping out at her family-owned bakery before starting her adult career as a computer programmer/systems analyst.

Dawn was named the 'most promising feminist under 35' by *New Statesman* magazine and was honoured as MP of the year at the 2009 Women in Public Life Awards. In 2020 she was recognized as one of the twenty-five most influential women in the UK by *Vogue*.

Dawn made history as the first elected Black female minister in the UK, serving in Gordon Brown's government.